Jack Lee-Flood
St Antony

NEW GEO WORKBOOK

Junior Certificate Geography

Liam Ashe

Kieran McCarthy

THE EDUCATIONAL COMPANY OF IRELAND

First published 1999

The Educational Company of Ireland
Ballymount Road
Walkinstown
Dublin 12

A member of the Smurfit Kappa Group plc

© 2009 Liam Ashe and Kieran McCarthy

Editor: Kate Duffy
Design and layout: Brendan O'Connell
Illustration: The Unlimited Design Company, Compuscript Limited, Helmut Kollars, Daghda
Cover design: The Design House

Ordnance Survey maps and aerial photographs
Based on Ordnance Survey Ireland Permit No. 8587
© Ordnance Survey Ireland/Government of Ireland

Acknowledgements
The authors and publisher wish to thank the following for permission to reproduce photos: Alamy, Corbis, European Photo Services Ltd (Peter Barrow) and irelandaerialphotography.com (John Herriot Photographic).

The authors wish to acknowledge their debt to the series editor Kate Duffy and designer Brendan O'Connell.

All rights reserved. No part of this publication may be reproduced, stored in a retrieval system, or transmitted in any form or by any means, electronic, mechanical, photocopying, recording or otherwise, without either the prior permission of the Publisher or a licence permitting restricted copying in Ireland issued by the Irish Copyright Licensing Agency, 25 Denzille Lane, Dublin 2.

The publishers have made every effort to trace and correctly acknowledge copyright holders. If, however, they have inadvertently overlooked any, they will be pleased to make the necessary arrangements at the first opportunity.

Any links to external websites should not be construed as an endorsement by EDCO of the content or view of the linked material.

05M15

CONTENTS

CHAPTER 1

THE EARTH

1.1 The Solar System

❶ Study the diagram below and answer the questions that follow.

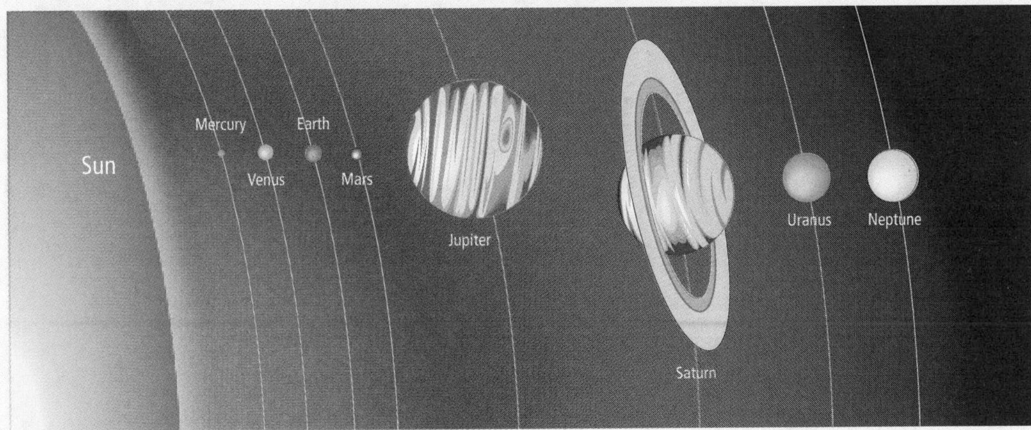

(a) How many planets are there in the Solar System? ______

(b) Name the planet that is closest to the sun. ______

(c) The sun is a planet. True or false? ______

(d) What name is given to Earth's journey around the sun? ______

(e) Why is Earth called the 'miracle planet'? ______

1.2 The structure of Earth

❶ Name the layers of Earth lettered A, B and C.

(a) ______

(b) ______

(c) ______

(d) Which layer is the hottest?

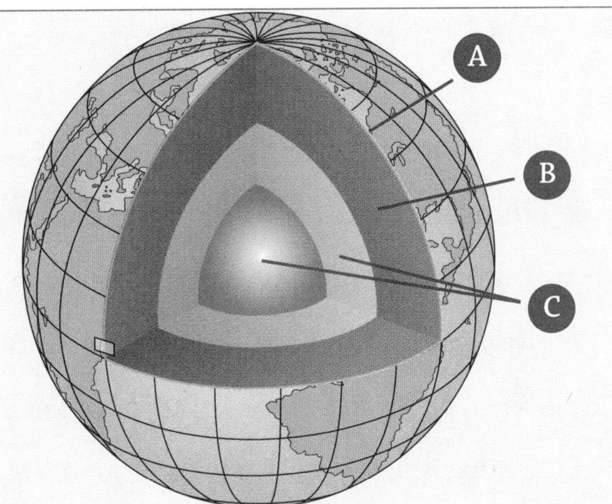

2 Complete each of the following sentences:

(a) The crust is the rockey surface around earth

(b) The mantle consists of semi-molten rock called magma

(c) Magma is molten or semi-molten

1.3 Plate tectonics

1 Examine the diagram below and answer the questions that follow.

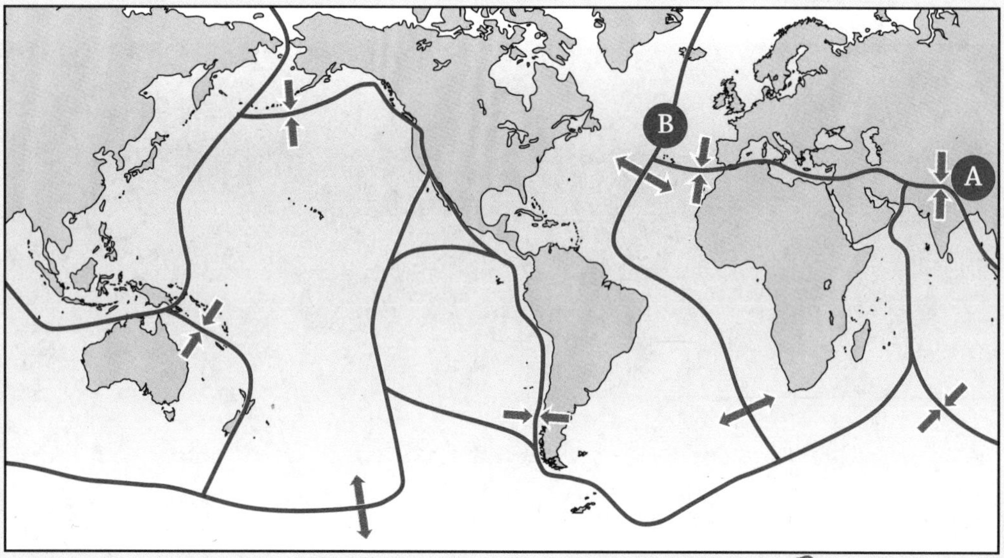

(a) On what plate does Ireland lie? Eurasion Plates

(b) Name the two plates colliding at A. Indian and Eurasion

(c) Name the two plates separating at B. Eurasion and American

(d) Name the plates that collide to form the Andes. Naza and American

(e) What country lies on the Mid-Atlantic Ridge? ~~Greenland~~ Iceland

2 Tick the box with the correct answer.

	True	False
(a) The Earth's crust consists of a number of plates.	✓	
(b) The plates move because of ocean currents.	~~✓~~	✓
(c) The original landmass was called Pangaea.	✓	
(d) New crust is formed at a constructive plate boundary.	✓	
(e) When plates collide, the lighter plate sinks.		✓
(f) Europe is slowly drifting towards America.	~~✓~~	

1.4 Volcanic activity

1 (a) What is the North Atlantic Ridge? Is a underwater mountain range

(b) Name the two plates that separate to form the North Atlantic Ridge.

(i) Eurasion (ii) American

(c) Which country forms part of the North Atlantic Ridge? Iceland

(d) Describe, with the aid of a diagram, how a mid-ocean ridge forms.

Mid-ocean ridge is an underwater mountain range. It is formed where two plates separate.

2 (a) Link each term below with its correct letter on the diagram.

Crater	B
Lava and ash flows	C
Mantle	e
Crust	F
Ash and gas cloud	A
Vent	D

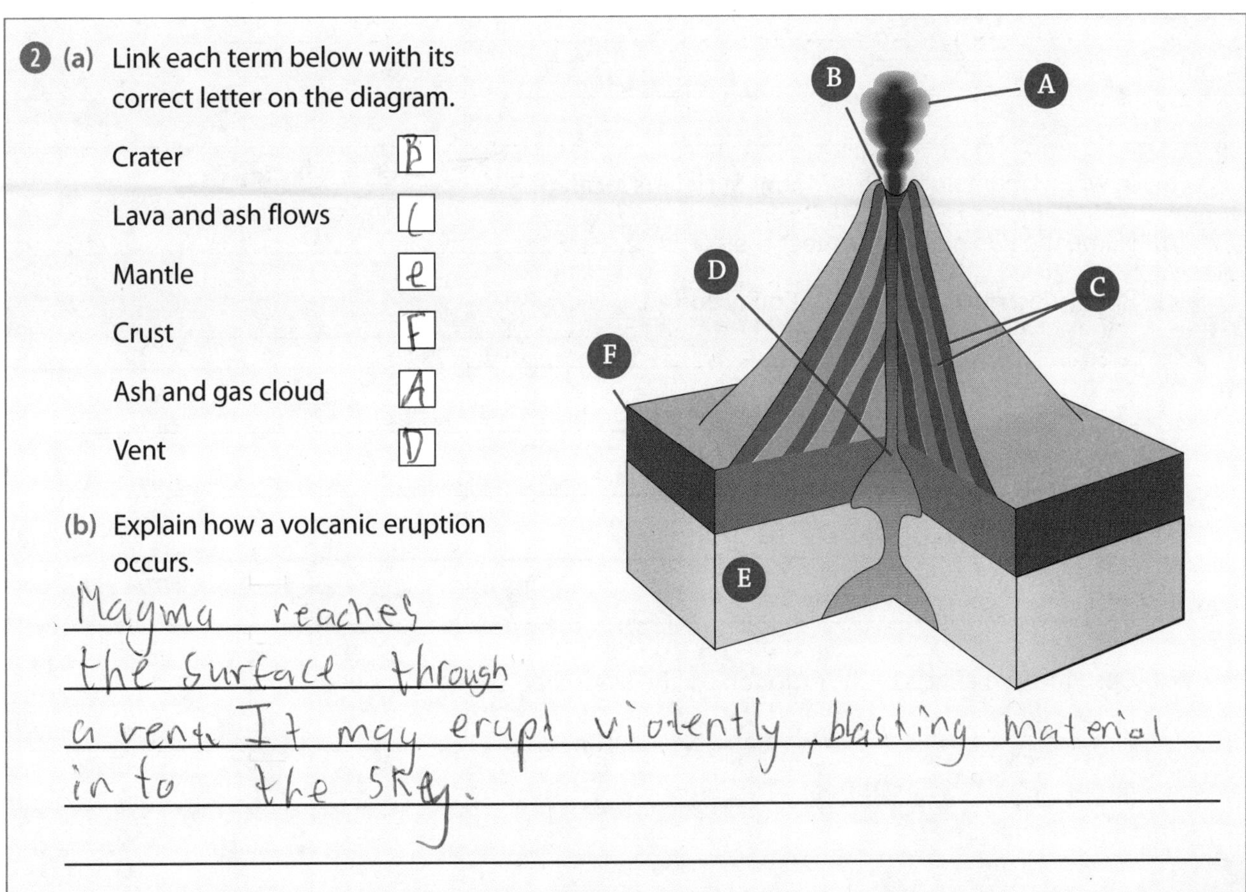

(b) Explain how a volcanic eruption occurs.

Magma reaches the surface through a vent. It may erupt violently, blasting material in to the sky.

3 (a) Circle the correct answer in each of the following statements:

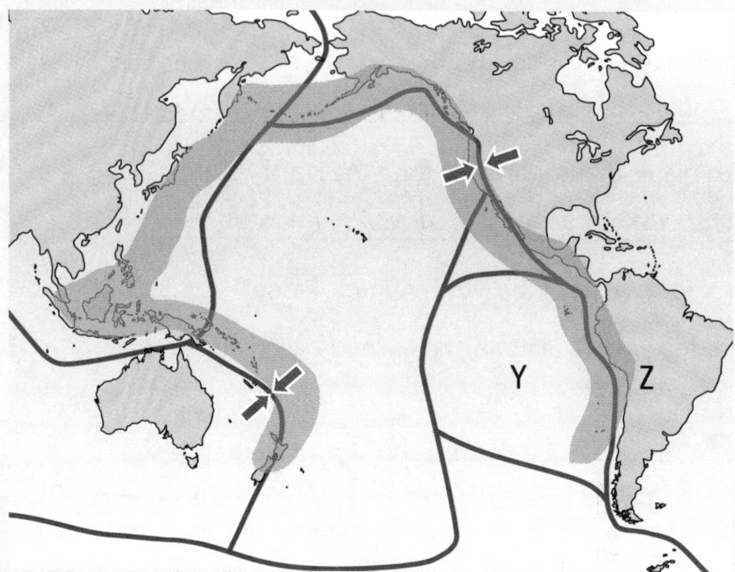

(i) The shaded area is the *Pacific Ring of Fire* / *the Pacific Ridge*.

(ii) The plate labelled Y is the *Nazca Plate* / *the Pacific Plate*.

(iii) The mountains labelled Z are called *the Andes* / *the Rockies*.

(iv) The shaded area is so called because it contains *many volcanoes* / *forest fires*.

(v) The map shows that crustal plates *collide* / *separate* along much of the shaded area.

(b) Name three volcanoes found along the Pacific Ring of Fire.

(i) Mt. Fuji (ii) Mt. St Helens (iii) Mt Pinatubo

4 (a) In what mountain range is Mount St Helen's located? ~~North America~~ The rockies

(b) Name the two plates that meet there. Eurasion and American

(c) Briefly describe how the eruption occurred.

It started when small lava and flows out of the volano a suddely a big cloud of ash and fire it soon turned into a tremedous volcanic eruption.

(d) Describe two effects of the eruption on the landscape.

(i) Melted snow and ice

(ii) Destroyed forest

1.5 Earthquakes

1 Circle the correct answer in each of the following statements:

(a) Earthquakes often occur at the *centre of* / *the edge* of the world's plates.

(b) Strong earthquakes occur in *Ireland* / *California*.

(c) Underwater earthquakes produce *tsunamis* / *tidal waves*.

2 (a) Link each term below with its correct letter on the diagram.

Term	Letter
Tremors	
Focus	
Fault	
Serious damage	
Crust	
Epicentre	
Minor damage	

A B C D E F G

3 (a) What are aftershocks?

____

(b) Why can aftershocks cause so much damage?

____

____

4 Circle the correct answer in each of the following statements:

(a) This instrument is used to measure the strength of an earthquake.

Seismometer / Richter Scale / epicentre / tsunami

(b) These are the shockwaves that occur during an earthquake.

Aftershocks / tremors / epicentres / seismometers

(c) This is the point in the Earth's crust where the earthquake starts.

Tsunami / focus / seismometer / epicentre

(d) This is the point on the Earth's surface where the tremors are strongest.

Epicentre / focus / tsunami / seismometer

5 In the case of any earthquake that you have studied:

(a) In what region or country did it occur? China

(b) What plates are in collision there? Indian / Eurashion

(c) Describe any two effects of the earthquake on the people of the region.

It ruens houses.

(d) How did the earthquake affect the landscape?

It might crack roads.

6 (a) What is a tsunami?

A Tsunami is a big wave.

(b) Why can it be so deadly?

It floods the towns and city. And electrisity can't work.

1.6 Fold mountains

1 Circle the correct answer in each of the following statements:

(a) Fold mountains are formed when plates *collide* / *pull* apart.

(b) Fold mountains are found at *the centre of* / *the edge* of the world's plates.

(c) The rocks are under *little* / *great pressure* and they *buckle* / *crack*.

(d) The rocks buckle upwards to form *downfolds* / *upfolds*.

2 Describe how fold mountains are formed.

Fold mountains are when two plates collide the rocks then buckle and crumple upwards.

3 Circle the correct answer in each of the following statements:

(a) The Andes are an example of *young / old* fold mountains and were formed as recently as *30 / 250* million years ago. They are *very high / quite low* because they *have been / have not yet been* worn down. Other examples include the *Alps / Scottish Highlands* and the *Caha / Rocky Mountains.*

(b) The mountains of Munster are much *older / younger* and were formed about *30 / 250* million years ago. Mountains that were formed during this period of folding are known as *Alpine / Armorican* fold mountains. They *have / have not* been severely worn down over the years.

4 Indicate whether each of the following statements is true or false by ticking the correct box.

	True	False
(a) Irish mountain ranges are as high as the Himalayas and Alps.	☐	☑
(b) Fold mountains are still forming in Ireland.	☐	☑
(c) Carrantuohill is the highest mountain in Ireland.	☑	☐
(d) The Alps are younger than the Galtee Mountains.	☑	☐

5 Examine the map of Ireland and, with the aid of an atlas, link the name of each fold mountain range with its correct letter.

Comeragh Mountains	D
Galtee Mountains	C
Magillicuddy's Reeks	B
Bluestack Mountains	J
Caha Mountains	A
Slieve Bloom Mountains	F
Ox Mountains	H
Twelve Bens (Pins)	G
Silvermines Mountains	e
Derryveagh Mountains	K

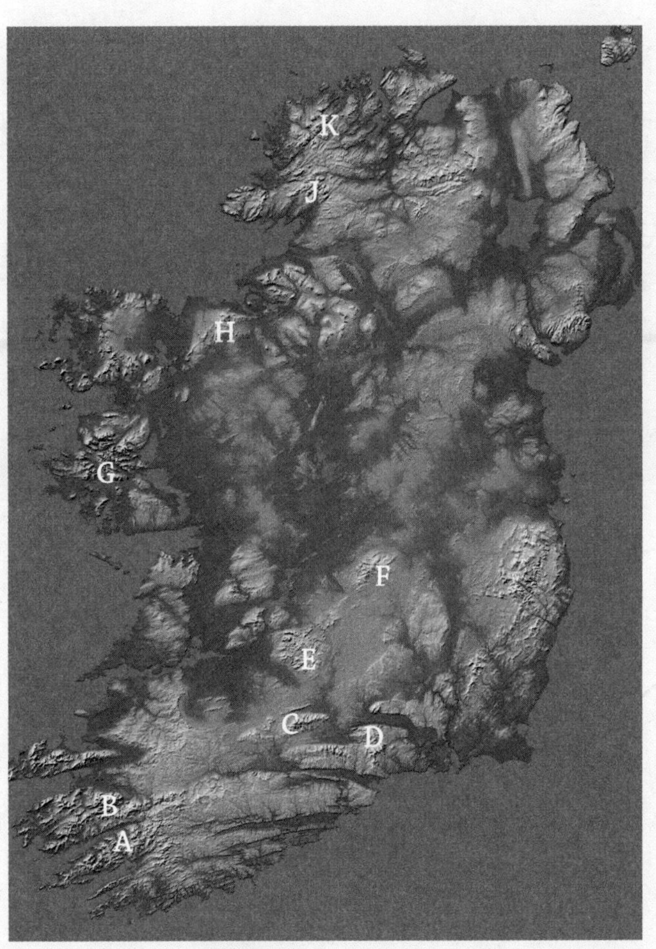

Revision crossword

Down

1 The Earth's shape is like one of these
2 Range of fold mountains in Munster
3 Layer made up of molten rock
4 Outer layer of Earth, made of solid rock
6 Mountain range in Sligo
9 Mountain range where Eurasian and African plates collide
10 The original large landmass
13 Period of folding that occurred 30m to 35m years ago
14 A mid-ocean ..... forms where plates pull apart
16 Shocks during an earthquake
18 The point where the earthquake begins
20 Magma that has reached the surface of the Earth

Across

5 Period of folding that occurred in Munster
7 The miracle planet
8 Hole in the crust through which magma erupts
10 Sections that make up Earth's crust
11 Giant wave that results from an underwater earthquake
12 Molten material in the mantle
15 Plate that collides with the American Plate to form the Andes
17 Continental ..... is where the plates move on the mantle
19 Country located on the Mid-Atlantic Ridge
21 Layer at the centre of the Earth
22 Cone-shaped mountain

Chapter 2

Rocks

2.1 What is rock?

1 (a) Name the three rock groups. slate
marble
limestone

(b) How are rocks grouped or classified? They are classified as colour, Hardess, Texture and Mineral content.

2 Identify one type of igneous rock and complete the following table.

Rock type	Granite
Description	Granite is used for work tops.
How formed	Granite is formed when molten magma forced its way into the crust.
Location in Ireland	wicklow mountains.
Benefit to people	worktop at home.

3 Identify one type of sedimentary rock and complete the following table.

Rock type	Sandstone
Description	Sandstone is light yellow.
How formed	Sandstone is formed when large amounts of sand were worn away from the surface of earth and transported by wind and river.
Location in Ireland	Munster Mountains
Benefit to people	

❹ Identify one type of metamorphic rock and complete the following table.

Rock type	Marble
Description	Marble is pure white in colour.
How formed	It is formed when molten magma forces its way into a body of limestone.
Location in Ireland	Cork.
Benefit to people	used in fireplaces.

❺ Examine the map of Ireland and identify the main rock type at each location.

A	Sand Stone
B	Lime Stone
C	basalt
D	Quartzite
E	granite
F	Shales

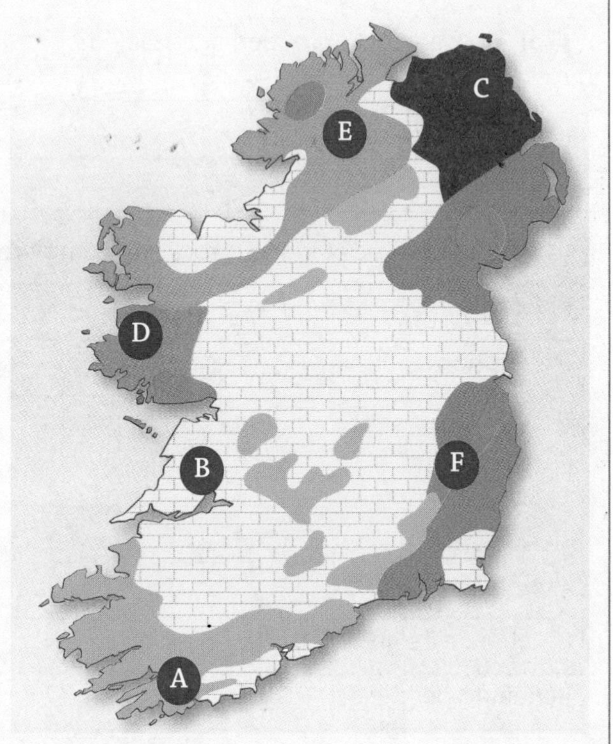

❻ Circle the correct answer in each of the following statements:

(a) Granite is an *igneous* / *sedimentary* rock found in *Cork* / *Wicklow*.

(b) *Sandstone* / *marble* is a metamorphic rock and has *large* / *small* crystals.

(c) *Limestone* / *granite* is formed from the remains of decayed *vegetation* / *sea creatures* and may contain *fossils* / *crystals*.

(d) Quartzite is an example of a *metamorphic* / *sedimentary* rock and was formed from *sandstone* / *limestone*.

(e) *Sandstone* / *basalt* is formed from layers of *sediments* / *molten magma* that were compressed and cemented together.

(f) The Giant's Causeway is formed of *granite* / *basalt* that formed when lava cooled *quickly* / *slowly* and solidified *on* / *beneath* the Earth's surface.

7 In the boxes provided, link each description in column 1 with its pair in column 2.

	Column 1
A	Ireland's most common sedimentary rock.
B	Metamorphic rock that was once sandstone.
C	Igneous rock found at the Giant's Causeway, Co. Antrim.
D	Coarse multi-grained igneous rock found in Wicklow.
E	A fossil fuel found in the Midlands of Ireland.
F	An ornamental metamorphic rock found in Connemara.

	Column 2
B	Quartzite
D	Granite
F	Marble
A	Limestone
C	Basalt
E	Peat

8 Complete the following table.

Resource	Use 1	Use 2
Natural gas	Energy	Raw Matereul
Sand and gravel	building	Matereal
Peat	Fact	Raw Matereal

9 Complete the following table.

Mining method	Advantage	Disadvantage
Offshore drilling	Easy	Pipes
Opencast mining	~~Qurete~~	Not freily
Shaft mining	Quick	Peep

10 Identify the natural resource at each location.

A	~~Shales~~ Gas Field
B	~~Limestone~~ Coal Field
C	Oil Field
D	Gas Field

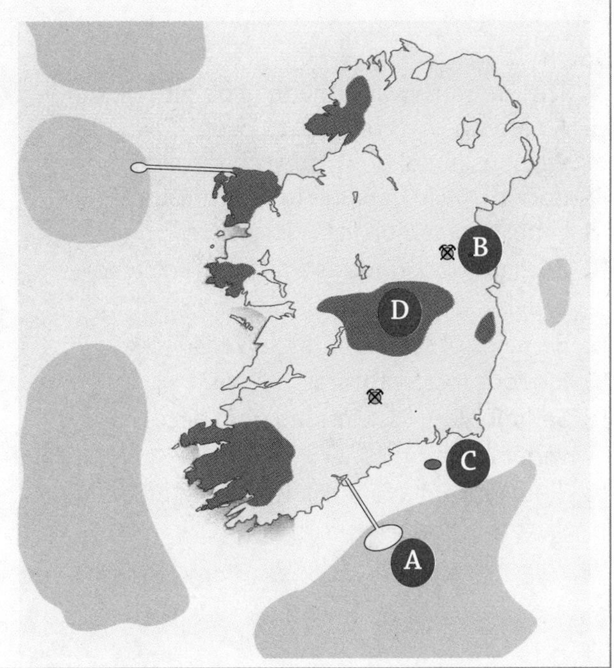

Revision crossword

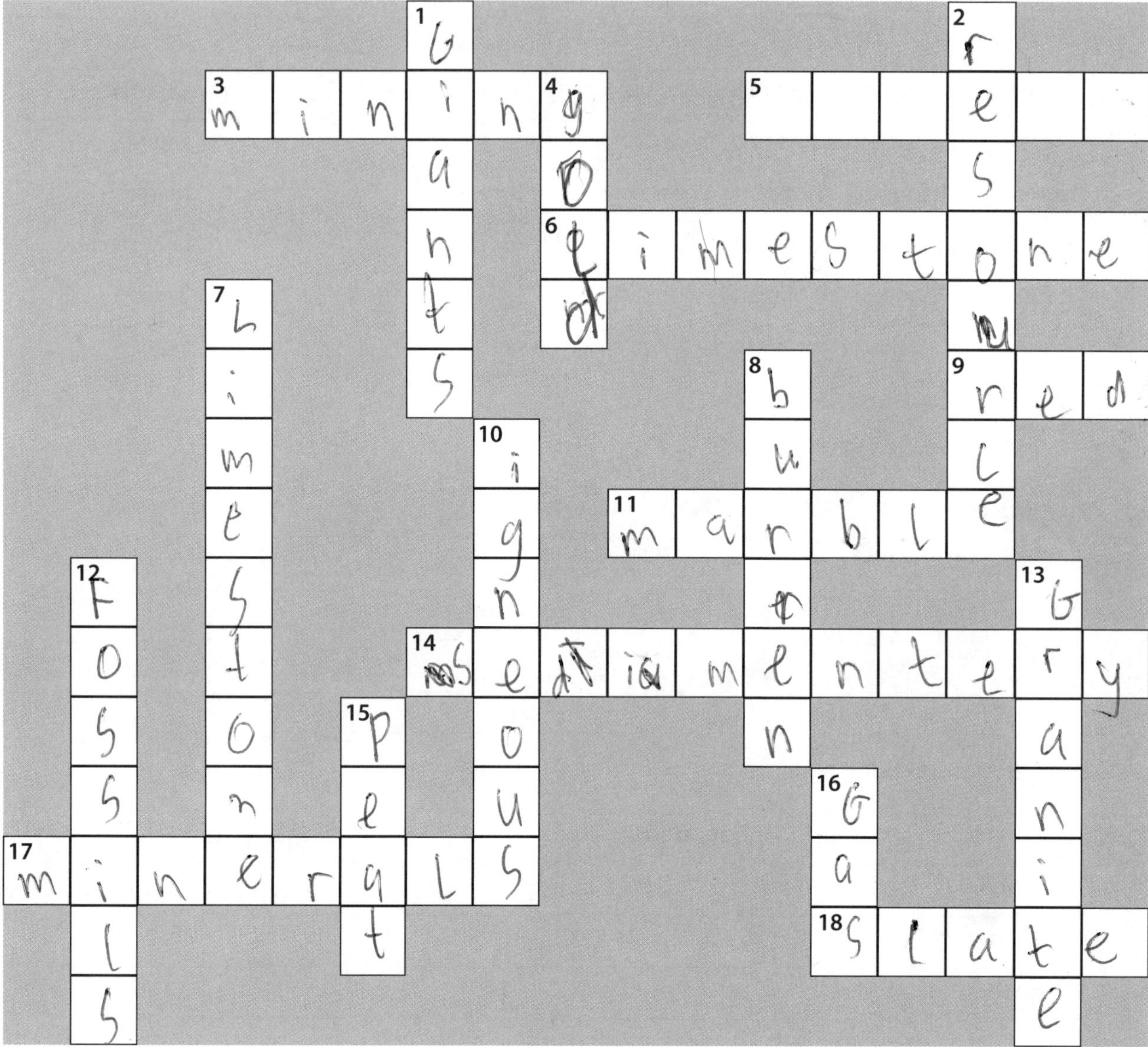

Down

1. The ...... Causeway is made of basalt
2. A natural .... is of value to people
4. Precious metal
7. Rock that allows water to pass through
8. Limestone region in County Clare
10. Rock group formed as a result of volcanic activity
12. Remains of skeletons preserved in rocks
13. Igneous rock with large crystals
15. Sedimentary rock formed from decayed vegetation
16. Energy source found in the ocean off Ireland

Across

3. A method of recovering minerals from Earth
5. This binds minerals together to form rocks
6. The most common rock in Ireland
9. One of the colours of sandstone
11. Metamorphic rock that can be red, green or white
14. Rock group formed from the remains of other rocks
17. Rocks are made of various combinations of these
18. This metamorphic rock is used as a roofing material

CHAPTER 3

SHAPING EARTH'S CRUST

3.1 Denudation: An introduction

❶ Link each explanation with the correct term from the following list:

erosion *weathering* *denudation*

Breakdown and decay of rocks	weathering
Breakdown of rock and removal of particles	erosion
Wearing away the rocks on the Earth's crust	denudation

❷ Weathering refers to:

Climate changes ☐ The breakdown of rocks ☑

Measuring temperature ☐ Removing soil and rock ☐

❸ Which of these is not a cause of erosion?

Sea ☐ Rivers ☐ Frost ☑ Ice ☐

3.2 Mechanical weathering

❶ Complete the flow chart, using the terms given below, to describe the freeze-thaw action.

Rock is put under pressure *Water freezes and expands*

Rock particles are broken off *Temperature drops below freezing point*

START Water in crack in rock → Temperature drops below freezing → water freezes and expands → Rock is put under pressure → Rock particles are brocke off → FINISH Scree gathers at foot of slope

❷ Circle the correct answer in each of the following statements:

(a) The photograph shows the result of *freeze-thaw* / *erosion*.
(b) This is an example of *chemical* / *mechanical* weathering.
(c) The rock pile produced is made of *fossils* / *scree*.
(d) This type of weathering is associated with *upland* / *lowland* regions.
(e) For freeze-thaw to occur, the temperature must *rise above and fall below* / *always stay below* / *never go below* freezing point.
(f) Freeze-thaw is most likely to occur in Ireland *throughout the year* / *in summer* / *in winter*.

3.3 Chemical weathering

❶ (a) Name the type of weathering that is active in the photograph.

~~Chemical weathering~~ Carbonation

(b) What evidence from the photograph indicates that weathering is taking place?

The chemical weathering is diging its way into the rock.

(c) Describe how it occurs.

When the rain, frost and hail are hiting it, it get weak and bits can break Off.

2 Examine the diagram below and identify each of the features lettered A to H.

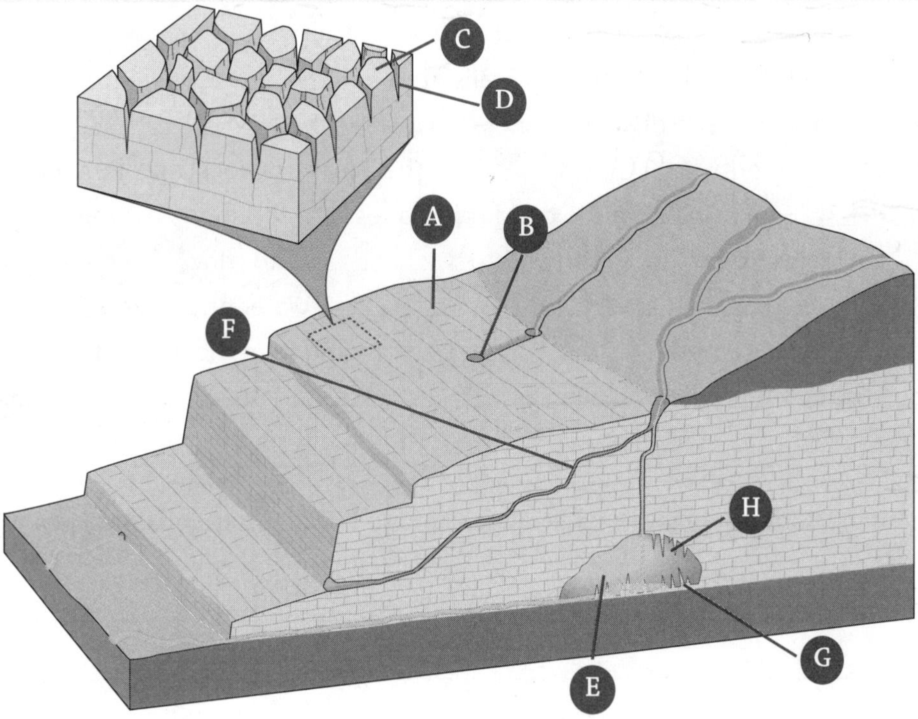

Clint	C	Cavern	E
Grike	D	Stalactite	H
Cave	F	Stalagmite	G
Swallow hole	B	Limestone pavement	A

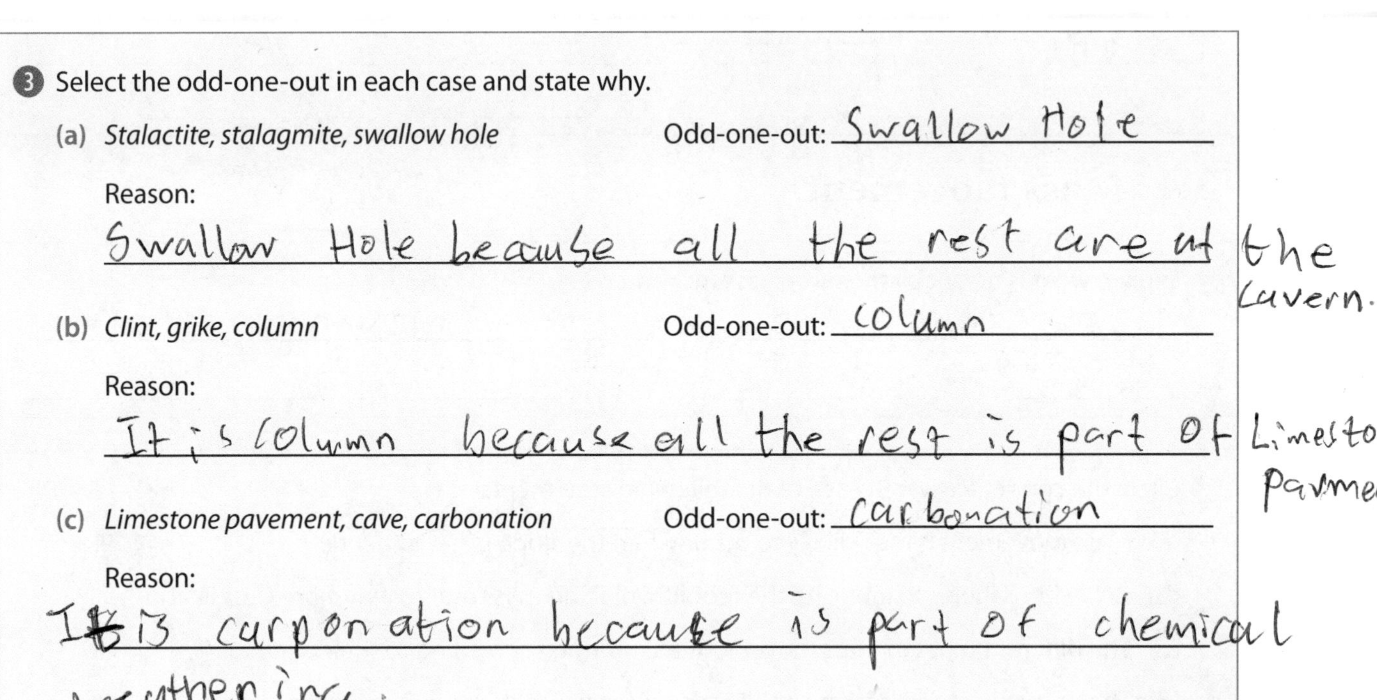

3 Select the odd-one-out in each case and state why.

(a) *Stalactite, stalagmite, swallow hole* Odd-one-out: Swallow Hole

Reason:

Swallow Hole because all the rest are of the cavern.

(b) *Clint, grike, column* Odd-one-out: column

Reason:

It is column because all the rest is part of Limestone pavement

(c) *Limestone pavement, cave, carbonation* Odd-one-out: carbonation

Reason:

It is carponation becauke is part of chemical weathering.

4 Fill in the blanks, using the words below.

carbon dioxide   carbonic   caves   clints   grikes   limestone   pillar
rivers   stalactites   stalagmites   swallow holes

Rainwater gathers ____________ as it falls through the atmosphere to form a weak ____________ acid. This acid dissolves minerals in rocks such as ____________. Joints in the rock are widened to form ____________. The blocks of rock that remain are called ____________. Some joints and bedding planes are opened to the extent that ____________ disappear through ____________ to flow underground. These underground streams cut passages called ____________. Water drips through the rock and may leave deposits of calcite called ____________ hanging from the roof of the cave. Similar deposits that build up on the ground are called ____________. If the stalactites and stalagmites join up, a ____________ is formed.

5 Many tourists visit the Burren to enjoy its wide range of attractions. Identify and describe any two of these attractions.

(a) ____________________

(b) ____________________

6 Describe two benefits and two problems of tourism in regions such as the Burren.

Benefits	Problems
1	1
2	2

3.4 Mass movement

1 Explain what is meant by the term mass movement.

____

2 Circle the correct answer in each of the following statements:

(a) Mass movement is more likely to occur when the slope is *steep / gentle*.

(b) *Water / frost* helps to lubricate the regolith, making mass movement *more / less* likely.

(c) The different types of mass movement are grouped according to their *material / speed*.

(d) The presence of vegetation can *slow down / speed up* the rate of mass movement.

3 Circle the correct answer in each of the following statements:

(a) The rapid movement of rock and soil down a slope is called soil

creep / landslide / bogburst / mudflow.

(b) The rapid movement of a mass of peat down a slope is called soil

creep / landslide / bogburst / mudflow.

(c) Which of the following is not influenced by heavy rainfall?

soil creep / landslide / bogburst / mudflow

(d) Which of the following is a slow form of mass movement?

soil creep / landslide / bogburst / mudflow

4 (a) Name the type of mass movement shown in the diagram: Soil creep

SOIL
ROCK

(b) How would you identify that it has taken place?

Yes because it has bent the tree broke the wall and you can see under the fence the ground

(c) Describe how it occurs.

The soil come down and breaks the fence and walls and even bends tree

5 Select one form of mass movement and describe its effect on people and their property.

(a) Type of mass movement: Mudflow

(b) Effects on people:

It kills people

(c) Effects on property:

~~It break walls, fences and trees and~~
~~It~~ kills people - It reaks houses and everything.

6 Complete the grid.

Type of mass movement	Speed	Material
Soil creep	Slow	Soil
Mudflow	Fast	Earth and rock (regolith)
Bogburst	Fast	Earth and rock
landslides	fast	Rivers of rock, soil and water

Revision crossword

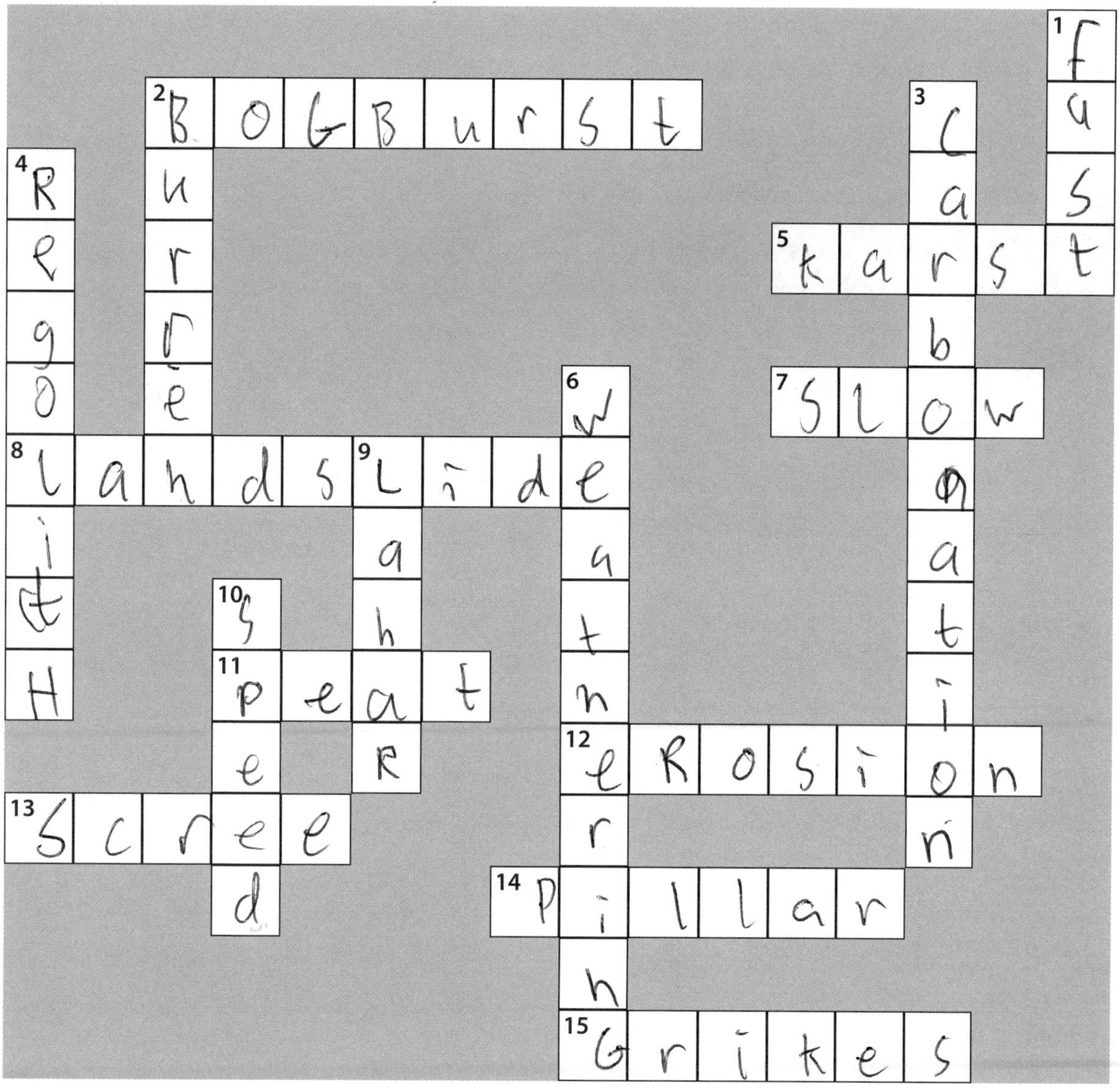

Down

1 Speed of landslides and mudflows
2 Ireland's best-known karst region
3 Type of chemical weathering in limestone regions
4 Loose material on the surface of the Earth
6 Breakdown and decay of rocks
9 Mudflow that contains volcanic ash and rock
10 How types of mass movement are grouped

Across

2 Mudflow containing peat and water
5 Landscape such as the Burren
7 Speed of soil creep
8 Rapid movement of regolith down a steep slope
11 Material in a bogburst
12 Breakdown of rocks and removal of particles
13 Rock pieces broken off by freeze-thaw
14 Formed when a stalactite joins with a stalagmite
15 Deep gashes between clints in a limestone pavement

3.5 Rivers: Shapers of our land

❶ Examine the diagram and link each letter with the correct feature.

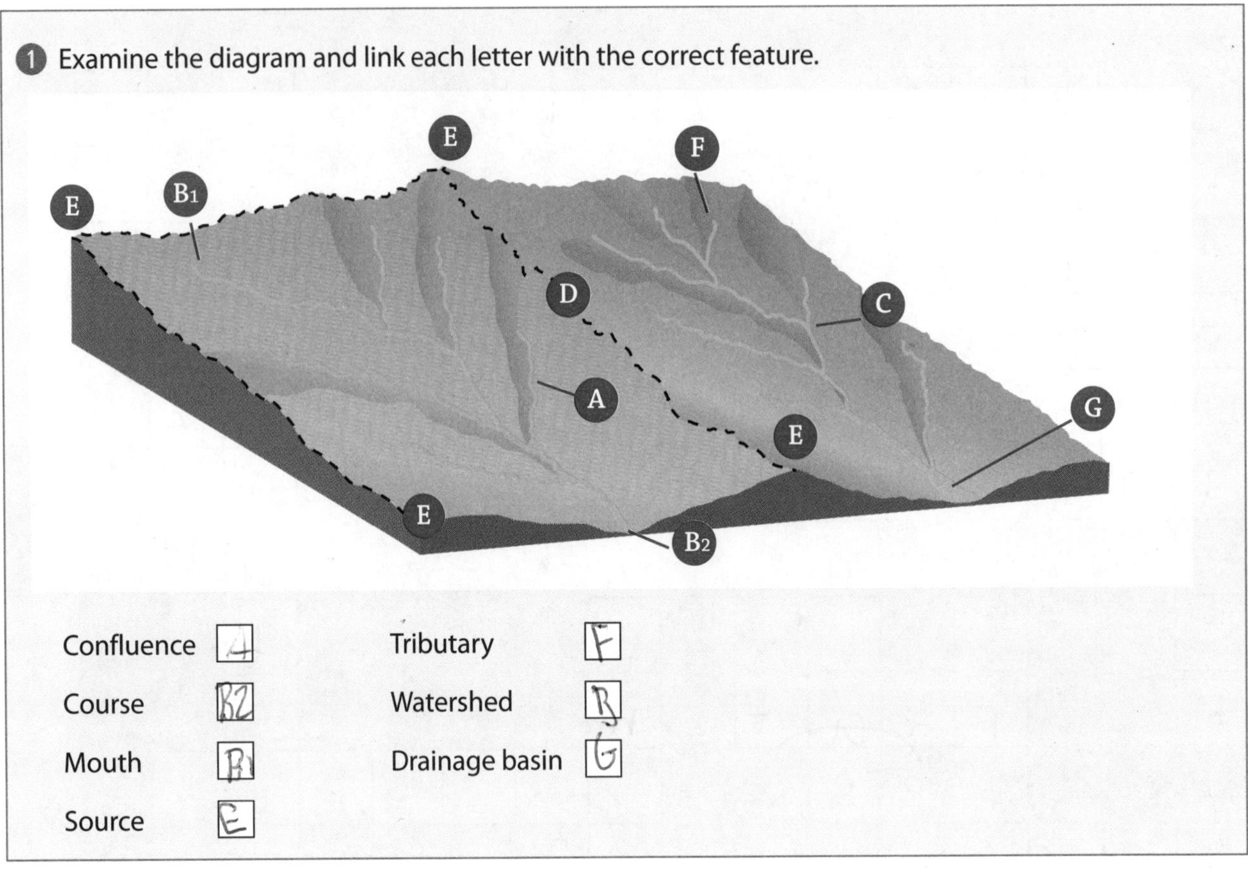

Confluence	A	Tributary	F
Course	B2	Watershed	B
Mouth	B1	Drainage basin	G
Source	E		

❷ Insert the river valley and gradient descriptions below into the appropriate boxes in the table.

Valley: *Very wide with flat floor* *Narrow with steep sides* *Wider with gently sloping sides*

Gradient: *Steep gradient* *Almost level* *More gentle*

Stage	Valley	Gradient
Youthful river	narrow floor	steep sides
Mature river	wide floor	gently sides
Old river	wide floor	gentleside

3 The diagram shows a river in its youthful (A), mature (B) and old (C) stages.

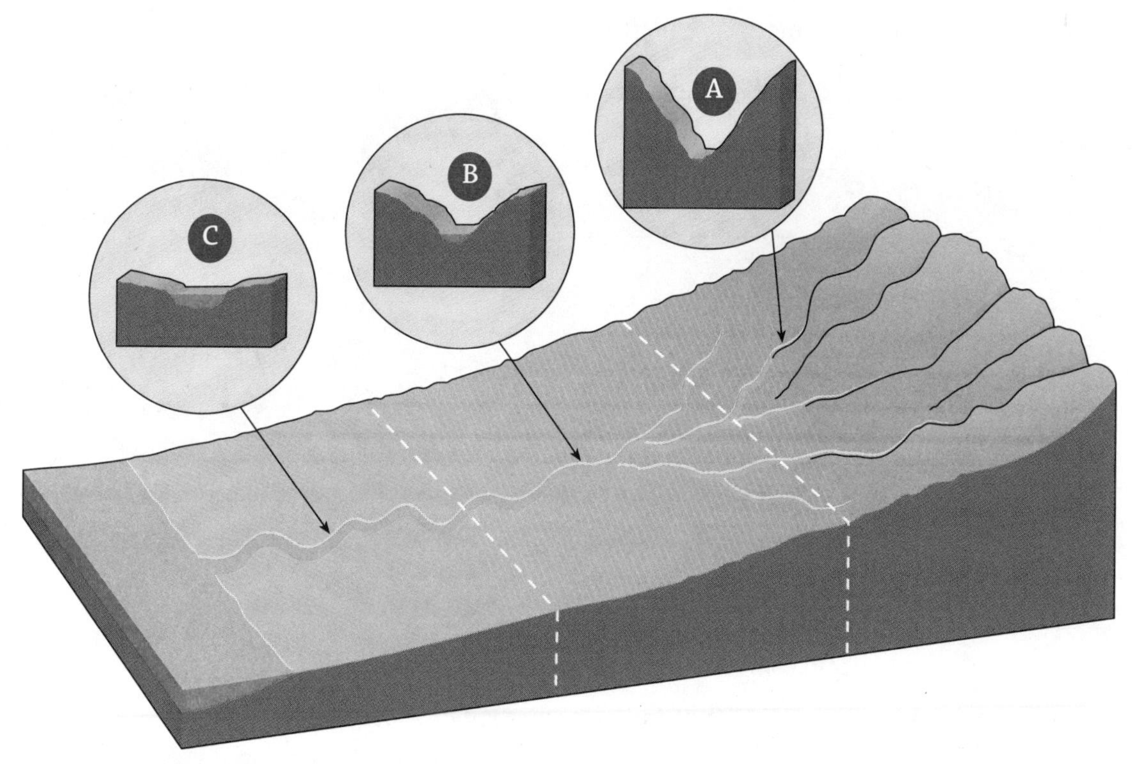

Circle the correct answer in each of the following statements:

(a) The river gradient is very gentle in *Diagram A / Diagram B / Diagram C.*

(b) The river flows fastest in *Diagram A / Diagram B / Diagram C.*

(c) Erosion from side to side is most common in *Diagram A / Diagram B / Diagram C.*

(d) Deposition is most common in *Diagram A / Diagram B / Diagram C.*

(e) Downward erosion is most common in *Diagram A / Diagram B / Diagram C.*

4 Link each term in column 1 with its matching pair in column 2. One match has been made for you.

Column 1	
A	Abrasion
B	Hydraulic action
C	Erosion
D	Solution

Column 2	
D	Rocks are dissolved by acid in the water.
	Wearing away of rock by the load material.
	The force of moving water.
	Breaking down and removing rocks.

5 (a) Name the feature in the diagram.

____

(b) Describe how it was formed.

____

____

____

____

____

(c) Name one example found in Ireland.

____

6 Circle the correct answer in each of the following statements:

(a) A river transports light particles of sediment by *solution* / *suspension*.

(b) The heaviest particles are *rolled along the bed* / *carried in the middle* of the river.

(c) The *sand-sized* / *dissolved* particles are transported by bouncing.

7 Examine the diagram and answer the questions that follow.

(a) The feature shown in the diagram is a:

Waterfall ☐

Estuary ☐

Delta ☐

Meander ☐

(b) The river is:

Eroding at A and at C. ☐

Depositing at B and at D. ☐

Eroding at A and depositing at C. ☐

Eroding at B and depositing at D. ☐

8 (a) Name a feature that results from deposition by rivers.

____

(b) Draw a labelled diagram of the feature.

(c) Describe how it was formed.

____

____

____

____

(d) Name one example found in Ireland. _______________________

9 Select the odd-one-out in each case and state why.

(a) *Hydraulic action, abrasion, transportation* Odd-one-out: _______________

Reason:

____

(b) *Waterfall, v-shaped valley, delta* Odd-one-out: _______________

Reason:

____

(c) *Oxbow lake, alluvium, waterfall* Odd-one-out: _______________

Reason:

____

(d) *Delta, floodplain, estuary* Odd-one-out: _______________

Reason:

____

3.6 Rivers and people

1 (a) Name one Irish river on which a dam has been built.

____

(b) List two advantages of the dam.

(i) ________________________

(ii) ________________________

(c) List two disadvantages of the dam.

(i) ________________________

(ii) ________________________

3.7 The sea: Builder and destroyer

1 Link each term in column 1 with its matching pair in column 2.

Column 1	
A	Waves
B	Fetch
C	Prevailing wind
D	Size of wave

Column 2	
	These can be constructive or destructive.
	In Ireland, it is has a south-westerly direction.
	The length of sea over which a wave passes.
	Influenced by the strength of the wind.

2 Link each term in column 1 with its matching pair in column 2.

Column 1	
A	Swash
B	Backwash
C	Constructive waves
D	Destructive waves

Column 2	
	These can cause erosion along the coast.
	Frothy water rushing towards the shore.
	Water that moves back down the shore.
	These can transport and deposit material.

3 Link each term in column 1 with its matching pair in column 2.

Column 1		Column 2	
A	Abrasion	C	Force of the waves hitting the coast.
B	Attrition	A	Rocks and stones used as a tool to erode.
C	Hydraulic action	D	Air trapped under pressure in cracks in rocks.
D	Compressed air	B	Rock particles are broken down and rounded.

4 Describe the formation of a cliff by completing the following flow chart, using the terms below.

overhang collapses *~~material is removed~~* *process is repeated*

~~coastline retreats~~ *notch is cut by erosion*

START Waves break at the coast → material is removed → coastline retreats → notch is cut by erosion → overhang colapses → process is repeated → leaving a cliff and wave-cut platform FINISH

5 Examine the diagram and link each landform with its correct letter in the diagram.

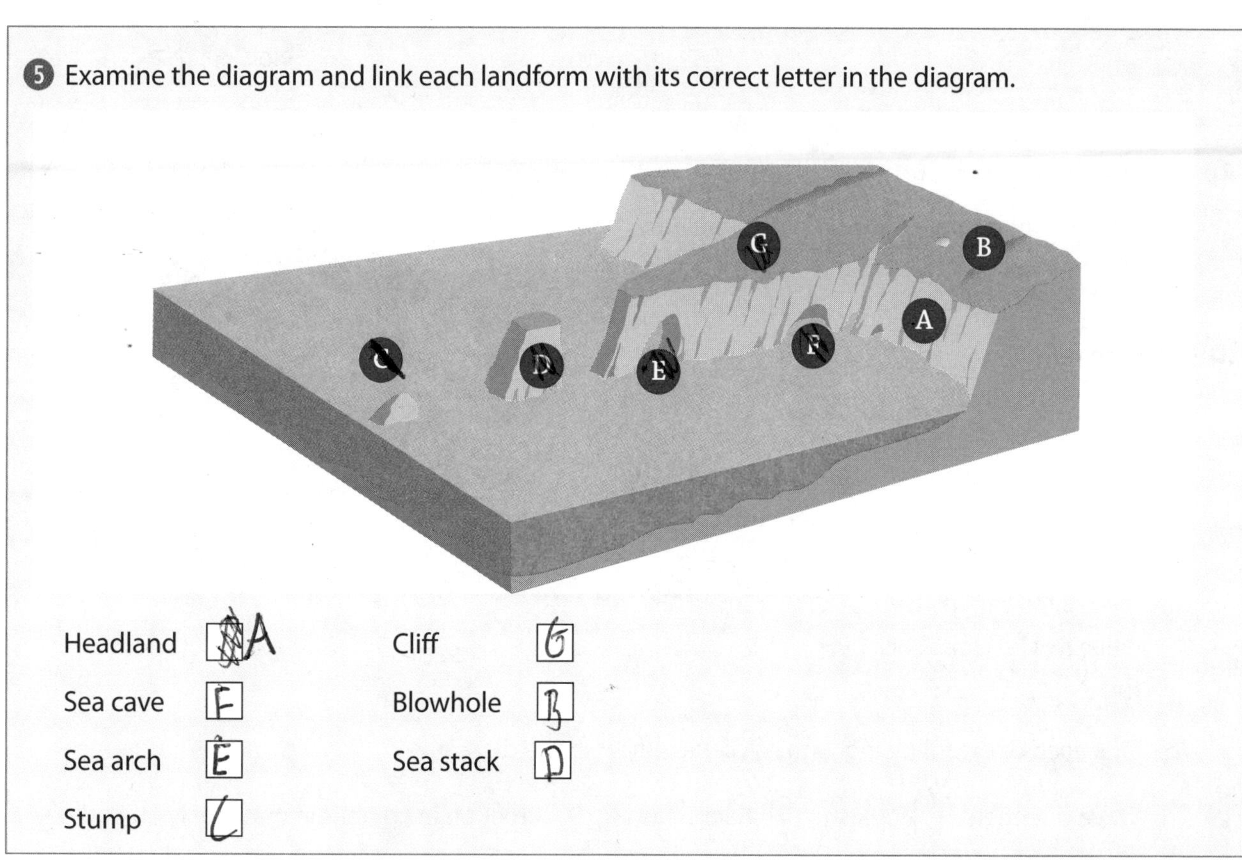

Headland	A	Cliff	G
Sea cave	F	Blowhole	B
Sea arch	E	Sea stack	D
Stump	C		

6 (a) Name one feature that results from erosion by waves.

Cliff

(b) Draw a labelled diagram of the feature.

Cliff
overhang
Notch
wave cut platform
Sea

(c) Describe how it was formed.

A clift is a vertical or steep on the coast. Destructive waves attack the coast and cut into the rock, eroding the notch.

(d) Name one example found in Ireland. Cliff of Mother in Co. Clare.

7 Examine the diagram and answer the questions that follow.

(a) Fill in the blank spaces using the following words:

angle *swash* ~~*longshore drift*~~

backswash ~~*along*~~

The diagram shows longshore drift where material is transported along the coast by waves. The waves meet the coast at an oblique angle. Material is moved forward by the ~~back swash~~ swash while it is brought back by the back wash.

A
B
C
D

(b) Link each of the following with its correct letter in the diagram.

Wave direction [C] Swash [D] Backswash [A] Direction in which the material is moved [B]

8 Examine the diagram and link each landform with its correct letter in the diagram.

Beach A

Lagoon E

Sand spit C

Tombolo D

Sand dune B

9 Link each term in column 1 with its matching pair in column 2.

	Column 1
A	Sandy beach
B	Storm beach
C	Tombolo
D	Sandspit
E	Lagoon
F	Sand dunes

	Column 2
F	Mounds of sand anchored by marram grass.
A	Sand and shingle stretching across a bay.
D	Deposited when waves are very strong.
B	Found between high and low tide levels.
C	Links an island to the mainland.
E	Bay cut off from the sea by a body of sand.

10 (a) Name one feature that results from deposition by waves. Beach

(b) Draw a labelled diagram of the feature.

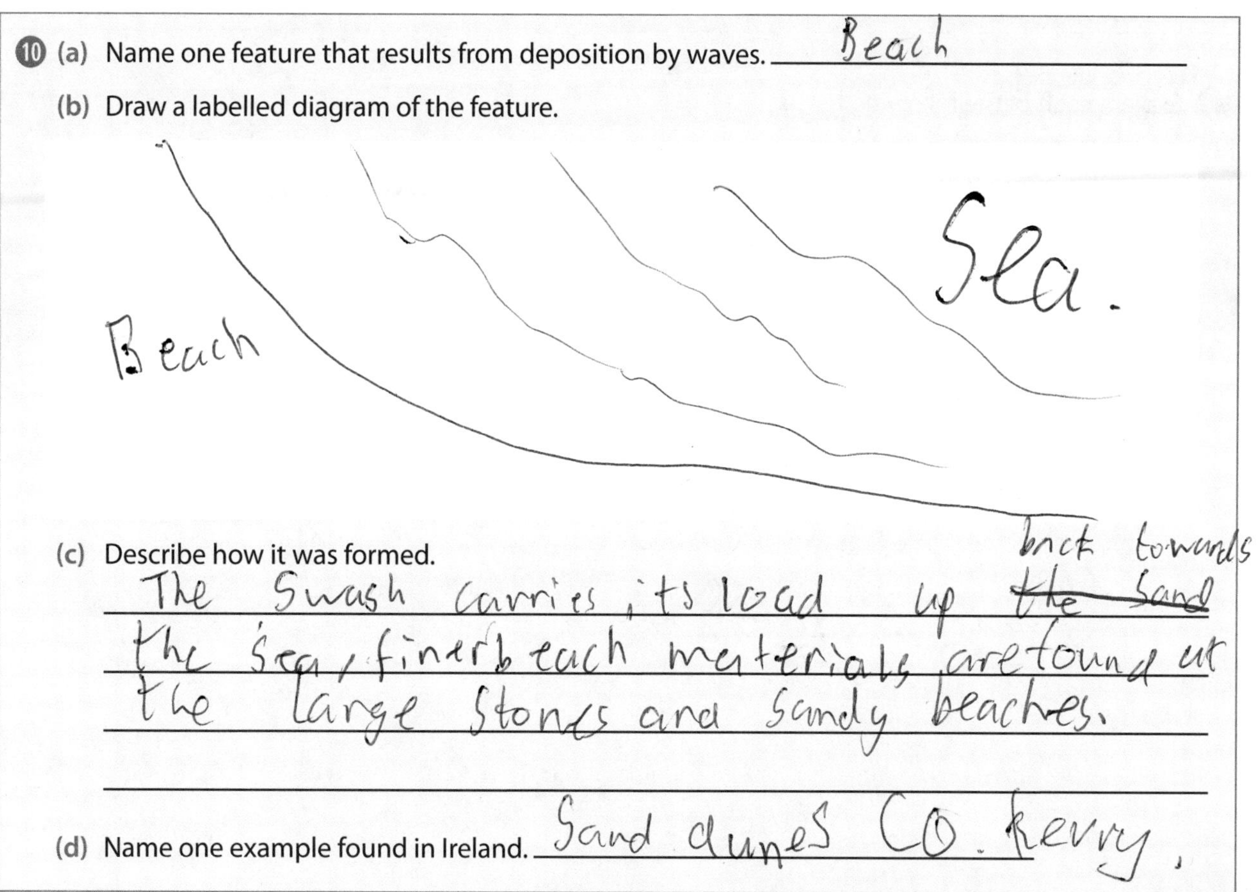

(c) Describe how it was formed.

The Swash carries its load up ~~the sand~~ back towards the sea, finer beach materials are found at the large stones and sandy beaches.

(d) Name one example found in Ireland. Sand dunes CO. Kerry.

3.8 People and the sea

1 Describe two ways by which people attempt to slow down or prevent coastal erosion.

(a) a dam

(b) man made levees

2 Describe two ways in which coastal areas are of benefit to people.

(a) Supplies 400 million Litres of water a day.

(b) The ESB Station, Built into the dam, generates hydro electricity.

3.9 Glaciation: The work of ice

1 Link each term in column 1 with its matching pair in column 2.

	Column 1
A	Ice Age
B	Glacier
C	Plucking
D	Abrasion

	Column 2
D	Rocks in glacier scratch the surface.
C	When land masses were covered by ice.
B	Rivers of ice moving down a mountain.
A	Glacier erodes by pulling rock away.

2 Explain each of the following terms.

Plucking:

As ice moves there is some friction between it and the ground.

Abrasion:

As the ice carries the plucked rocks away they scrape or scratch the rock surface over which the glacier passes.

3 Examine the diagram and link each landform with its correct letter in the diagram.

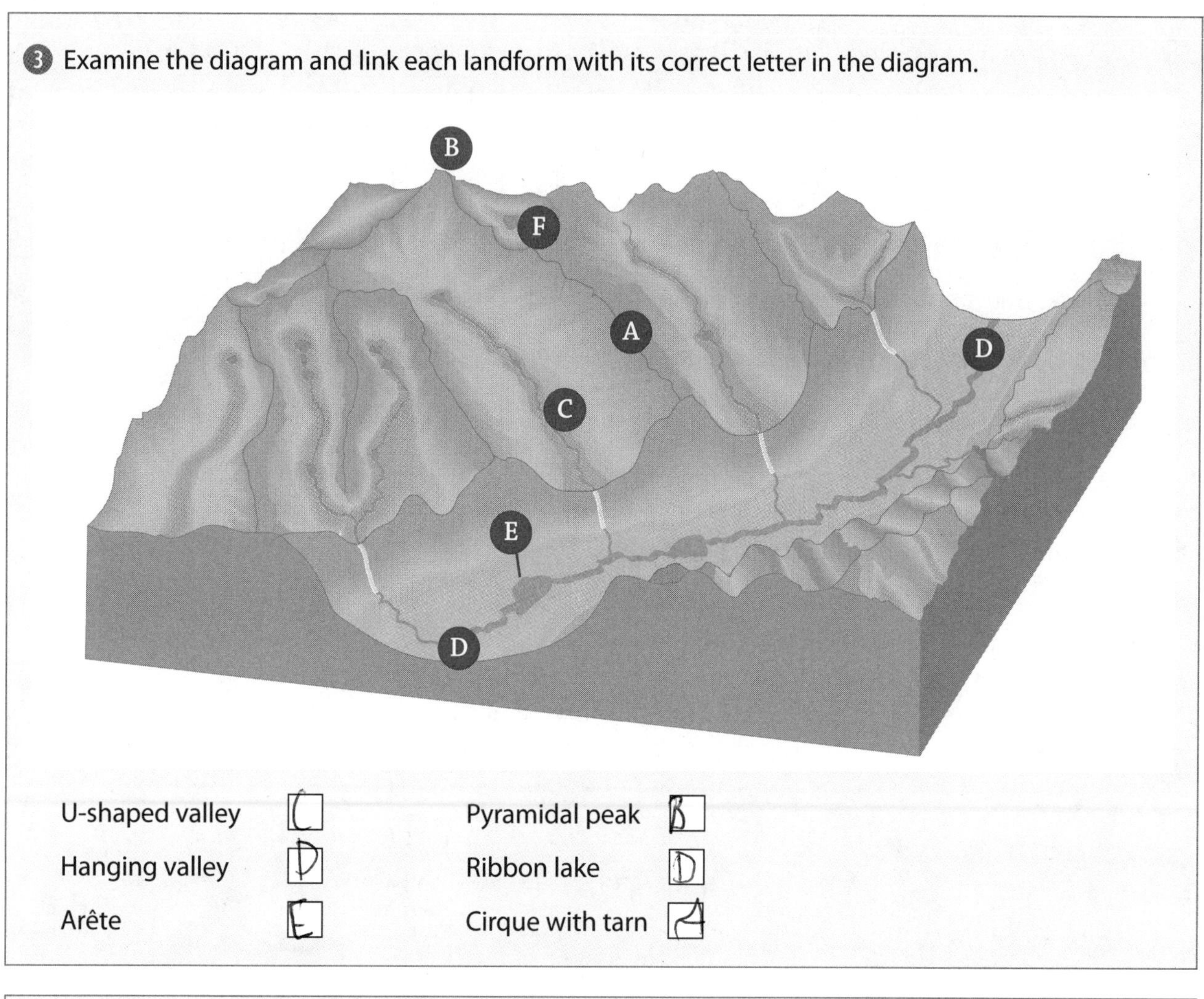

U-shaped valley	C	Pyramidal peak	B
Hanging valley	D	Ribbon lake	D
Arête	E	Cirque with tarn	A

4 (a) Select any one landform from those named in question 3. Fiords

(b) Describe how it was formed.

Fiords are any ~~ton~~narrow inlets that are very ~~steep~~ deep and have steep sides.

5 Link each term in column 1 with its matching pair in column 2.

Column 1	
A	Cirque
B	U-shaped valley
C	Arête
D	Hanging valley
E	Ribbon lake
F	Fiord

Column 2	
e	Hollow on valley floor, scooped out by ice.
B	Tributary glaciated valley.
a	Steep-sided hollow, the birthplace of a glacier.
F	Glaciated valley drowned by rising sea levels.
D	Glaciated valley has steep sides and flat floor.
C	Narrow, steep-sided ridge found between two cirques.

6 Solve each of the following clues. Each answer refers to deposition of glacial material.

(a) Cluster of egg-shaped hills

	U				N	

(b) Long ridges of sand and gravel

	S			R	

(c) Mixture of clay, silt, rocks and stones

B						C			

(d) Rocks transported and deposited by ice

	R	R					

(e) Plain with a covering of sands and gravels

	U				S	

(f) Lateral, medial or terminal

M						E

7 (a) Name one feature that results from deposition by glaciers.

____

(b) Draw a labelled diagram of the feature.

(c) Describe how it was formed.

____

____

____

____

(d) Name one example found in Ireland. ______________________________

8 Select the odd-one-out in each case and state why.

(a) *Cirque, drumlin, U-shaped valley* Odd-one-out: Drumlint

Reason: because the rest are land forms of glacial errosion

(b) *Esker, erratic, fiord* Odd-one-out: ______

Reason: because the rest are lanforms of melted water

(c) *Drumlin, plucking, abrasion* Odd-one-out: Drumlin

Reason: Plucking and abrasion are part of ice erodeing.

(d) *Esker, fiord, Ice Age* Odd-one-out: fiord

Reason: A fiord is a long narrow inlet.

3.10 Glaciation and human activity

1 Describe one benefit of glaciation on the Irish landscape.

hydroelectricity the steep slopes and water supply availible in the cirque has been used to generate hydroelectricity.

2 Describe one disadvantage of glaciation on the Irish landscape.

Enviromental impact like removed mus of the soil covered.

Revision crossword

Down

1 A steep or vertical slope found at the coast
2 Build-up of sand and shingle between high and low water marks
3 Material transported on, in, or in front of a glacier
5 Feature where a river flows over a vertical slope
6 Fan-shaped deposits where a river enters the sea
9 This type of wave helps build up the coastline
11 This forms after a sea cave but before a sea stack (3, 4)
12 Raised banks of alluvium along the old stage of some rivers
14 Low walls that reduce longshore drift
16 High ground that separates two river basins
17 A drowned U-shaped valley

Across

1 A large hollow, birthplace of a glacier
2 A wide opening between two headlands
4 Land on either side of a river with a covering of alluvium
7 Erosion where ice pulls rocks from the ground
8 The length of sea over which a wave travels
10 Ridge of sand and gravel deposited by glacial meltwater
13 This is a tributary valley to the main glaciated valley
15 Steep, narrow ridge between two cirques
18 Waves trap air in cracks in the rocks (10, 3)
19 Lake formed when a loop of a meander is cut off
20 Barriers that control the flow of water in a river
21 Egg-shaped groups of hills
22 Caused when a river bursts its banks

CHAPTER 4

THE RESTLESS ATMOSPHERE

4.1 The atmosphere

1 The atmosphere is a mixture of gases. (*Tick the odd-one-out.*)

Nitrogen ☐ Oxygen ☐ Ozone ☐ Methane ☐

2 The lower layer of the atmosphere is called the: (*Tick the correct box.*)

Radiation ☐ Troposphere ☐ Gas ☐ Hemisphere ☐

3 True or false:

		True	False
(a)	Oxygen is the main gas of the atmosphere.	☐	☐
(b)	The atmosphere contains minute particles of dust.	☐	☐
(c)	Most gases are found in the upper layers of the atmosphere.	☐	☐
(d)	The atmosphere is not necessary for life on Earth.	☐	☐

4.2 The heat machine

1 Fill in the blanks, using the words below.

high gases latitude atmosphere light Earth's surface equator heat

The sun is a mass of burning ______________ that provides us with ______________ and ______________. About 50 per cent of this heat is absorbed by the ______________, while 25 per cent is absorbed by the ______________.

The amount of heat received from the sun varies with the ______________ of a particular place. Places near the ______________ receive more heat than places with ______________ latitudes.

2 Circle the correct answer in each of the following statements:

(a) Places that are close to the equator are said to be in the *low / high* latitudes.

(b) The sun heats the Earth *equally / unequally*.

(c) The sun's rays shine directly on the surface of Earth at the *poles / equator*.

(d) In the northern hemisphere, winter is *warmer / colder* than summer because the northern hemisphere is tilted *towards / away* from the sun.

4.3 Wind: The atmosphere on the move

1 Circle the correct answer in each of the following statements:

(a) Warm air is *lighter / heavier* than cold air and so it *rises / sinks*.

(b) Air moves from areas of *low / high* pressure to areas of *low / high* pressure.

(c) Winds blowing from the direction of the equator are *warm / cold* winds.

(d) The wind that blows more frequently from one direction than any other is called the *prevailing / fetch* wind.

2 Examine the diagram and link each term with its correct letter.

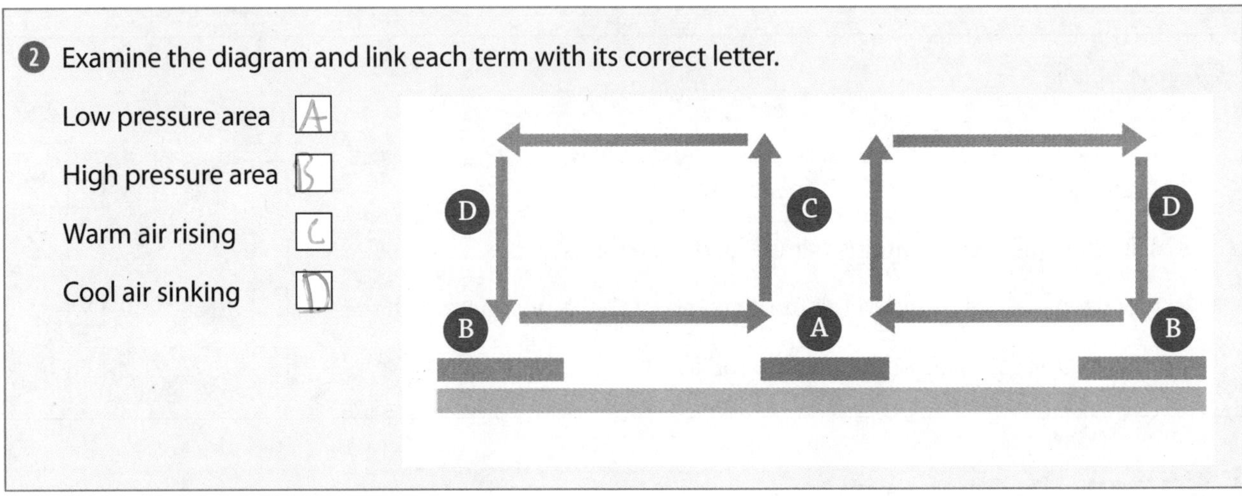

3 Explain each of the following terms:

(a) Atmospheric pressure:

____

____

(b) Prevailing wind:

____

____

(c) Coriolis effect:

____

____

4 Examine the diagram and circle the correct answer in each statement:

(a) The line of latitude at A is the *Tropic of Cancer / equator / Tropic of Capricorn*.

(b) The winds at B tend to *warm / cool* the areas over which they blow.

(c) The winds at C are called the *Trade Winds / Anti-Trade Winds*.

(d) D is a region of *high / low* atmospheric pressure.

(e) The area of low pressure at E is known as the *Horse Latitudes / Doldrums*.

(f) The winds that blow over Ireland are called the *Trade / Anti-Trade winds*.

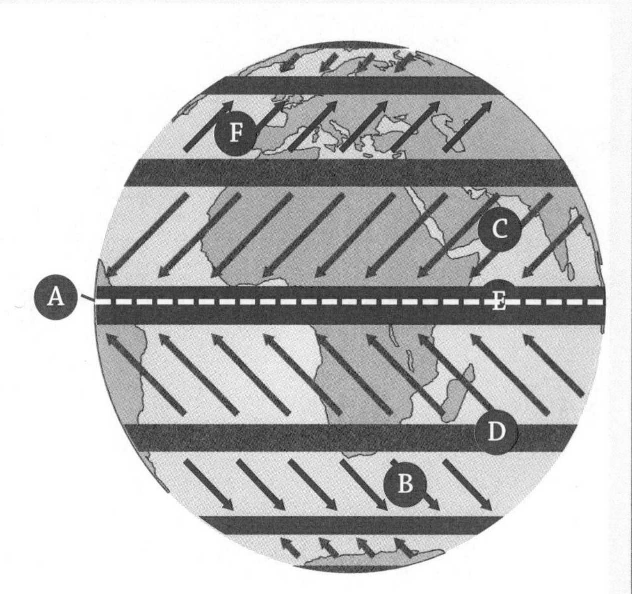

4.4 Ocean currents

1 Circle the correct answer in each of the following statements:

(a) Ocean currents result from the *equal / unequal* heating of the Earth's surface.

(b) The movement of ocean currents is also influenced by *winds / weather*.

(c) Currents that flow away from the equator are called *warm / cold* currents.

(d) Ocean currents in the northern hemisphere flow in a *clockwise / anti-clockwise* direction.

2 Examine the diagram about North Atlantic currents and complete the table, using the names of the currents below.

Canaries Current
North Atlantic Drift
Gulf Stream
Labrador Current

	Name of current	Warm or cold
A	Gulf Stream	warm
B	Labrador Currents	Cold
C	Canaries Current	cold
D	North Athlantic Drift	Warm.

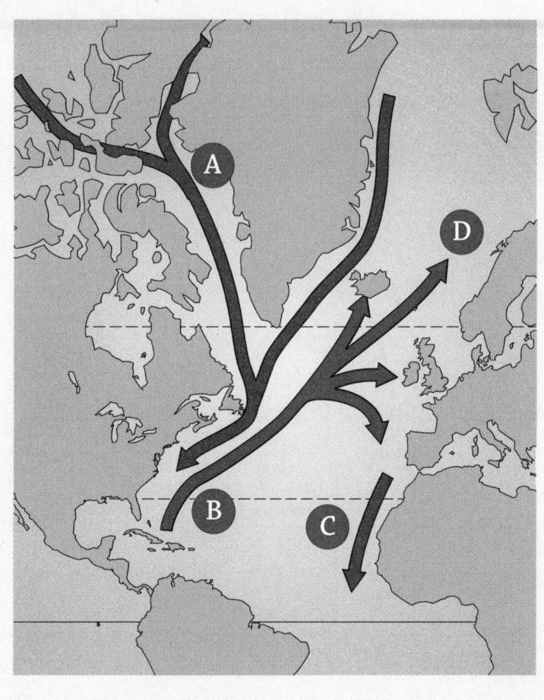

3 Describe any one effect of the North Atlantic Drift on Western Europe.

____

4 Describe any one effect of the Canaries Current on North Africa.

____

4.5 Air masses and weather systems

1 Explain each of the following terms:

(a) Air mass

____

____

(b) Front

____

____

2 Study the diagram and select A or B as the correct answer in each case.

Polar air mass ☐

Tropical air mass ☐

Brings hot summers ☐

Brings cold weather ☐

Brings winter showers ☐

Brings clear skies ☐

A

B

3 Complete the following table to describe the conditions that occur at a front.

Condition	Warm front	Cold front
Precipitation		
Wind speed		
Temperature		

4 Circle the correct answer in each of the following statements:

(a) A depression has an area of *high / low* pressure at its centre because of *ascending / descending* air.

(b) A depression forms where warm and cold *weather / fronts* develop.

(c) The warm sector contains *warm / cold* air and is almost surrounded by *warm / cold* air.

(d) Winds blow towards the centre of the depression in an *anticlockwise / clockwise* direction.

(e) Depressions are associated with weather that is *clear / cloudy* and *wet / dry* and *calm / windy*.

5 Which of the following sets of answers best describes an anticyclone? (*Tick the correct box.*)

(a) High pressure centre, clear skies, strong winds, warm nights ☐

(b) High pressure centre, cloudy skies, light winds, warm nights ☐

(c) Low pressure centre, clear skies, strong winds, cold nights ☐

(d) High pressure centre, clear skies, light winds, cold nights ☐

6 Examine the weather map and answer the following questions.

(a) Link each term with the correct letter.

Low pressure centre ☐

High pressure centre ☐

Isobar ☐

Reading in millibars ☐

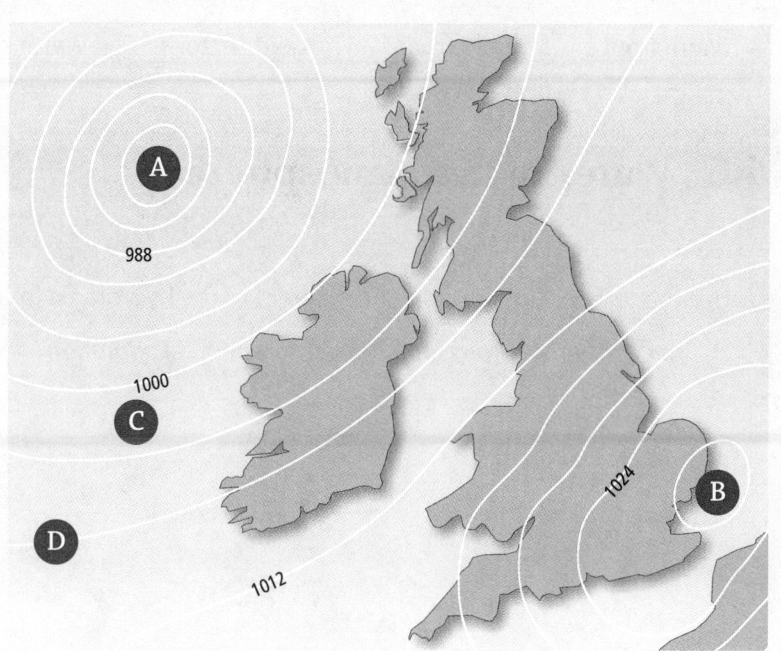

(b) Refer to the weather map and circle the correct answer in each statement:

(i) Ireland is affected by a *south westerly / north easterly* wind.

(ii) South-east England has *sunny / cloudy* weather.

(iii) Winds over Scotland are *strong / slack*.

(iv) The atmospheric pressure at B is just above *1020 / 1028* millibars.

(v) There is *wet and windy / warm and dry* weather to the north west of Ireland.

(vi) Winds to the north west of Ireland are *strong / slack*.

(vii) The atmospheric pressure near Dublin is *1004 / 1008* millibars.

7 Examine the diagram and link each term with the correct letter.

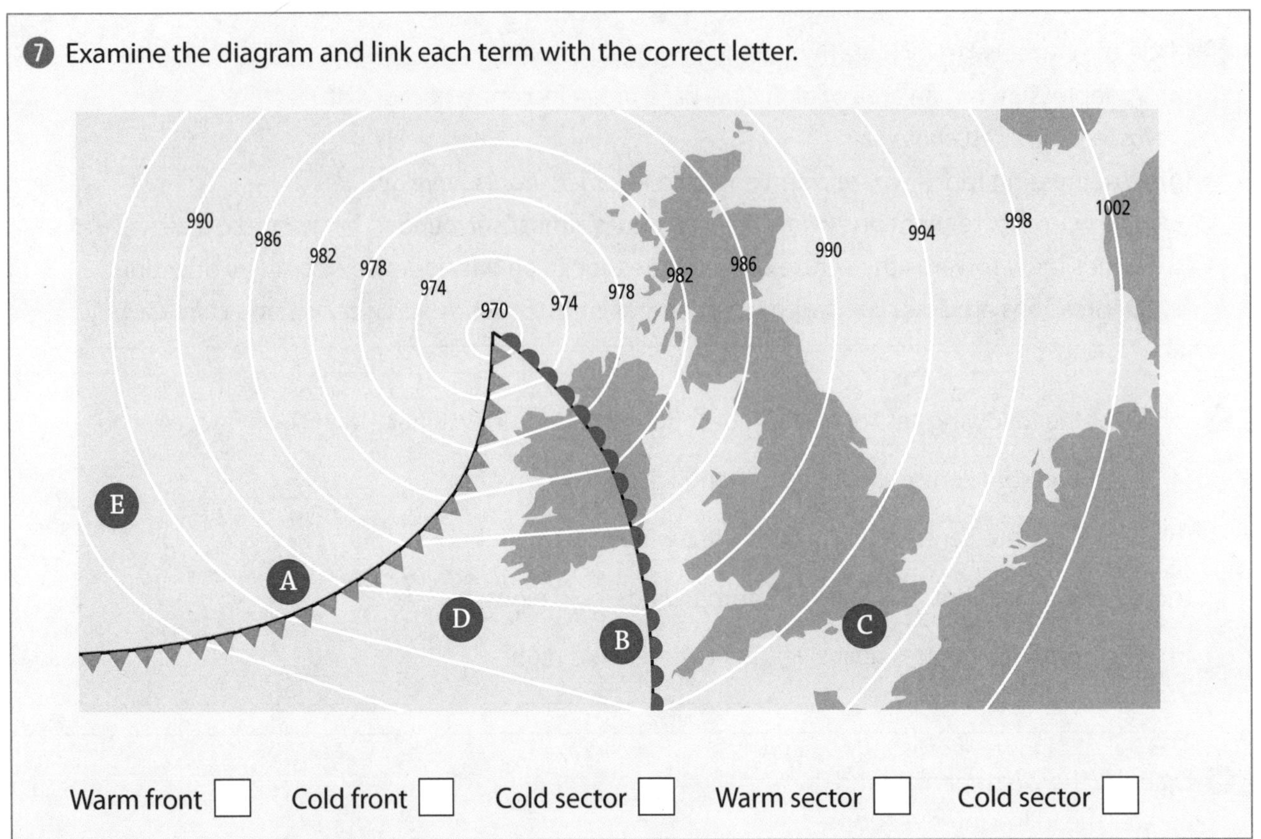

Warm front ☐ Cold front ☐ Cold sector ☐ Warm sector ☐ Cold sector ☐

4.6 Water in the atmosphere

1 Use the terms below to label the diagram of the hydrologic (or water) cycle.

condensation *precipitation* *storage* *evaporation* *run-off* *wind*

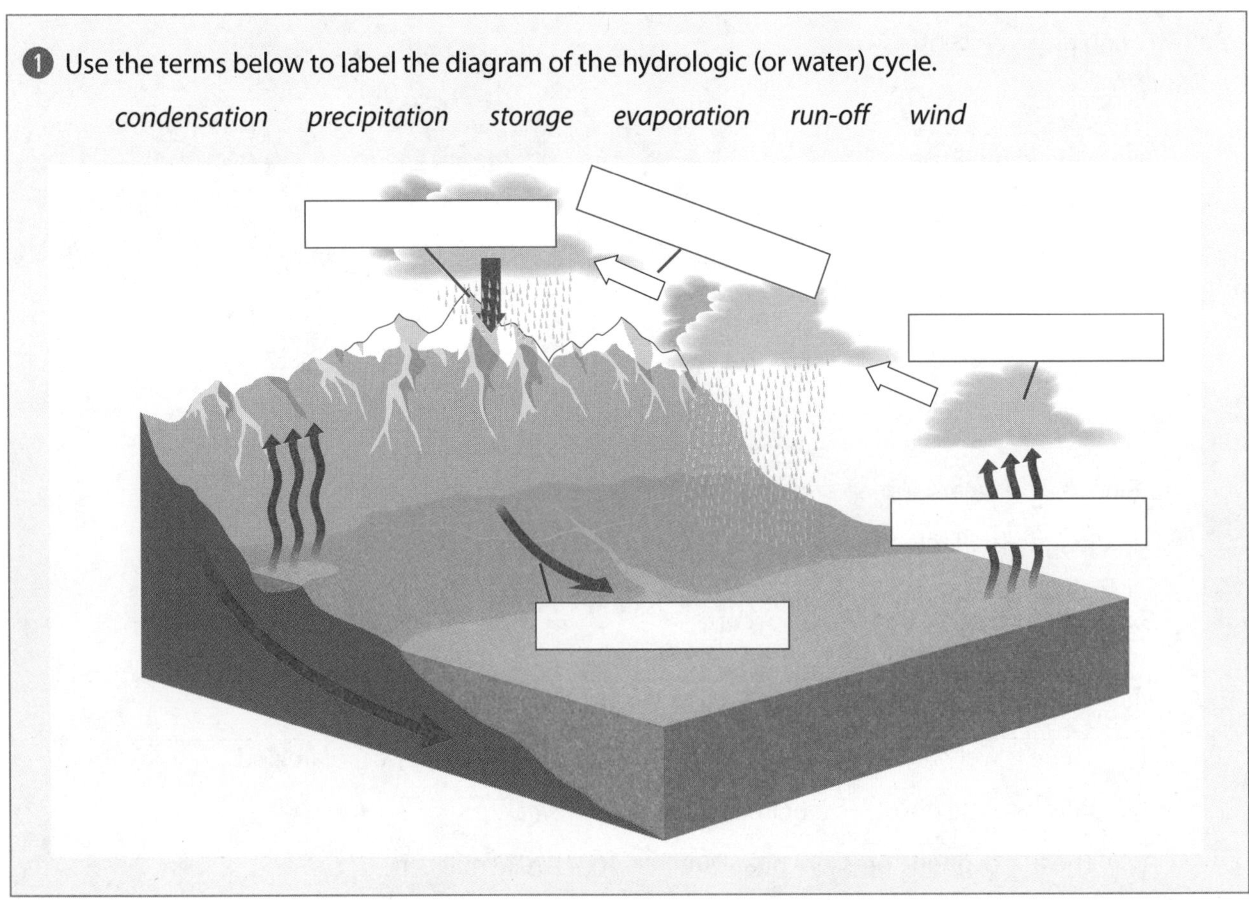

❷ Link each term in column 1 with its matching pair in column 2. One match has been made for you.

Column 1	
A	Precipitation
B	Evaporation
C	Saturation
D	Transpiration
E	Condensation
F	Hydrological cycle

Column 2	
D	Moisture from plant life.
	Relative humidity is 100%.
	Results in formation of clouds.
	Includes rainfall, snow, dew and frost.
	Also called the water cycle.
	Heat changes water to a vapour.

❸ Complete the following table about cloud types.

Cloud type	Altitude	Weather
Stratus		
	High altitude	
		Heavy rain and showers

❹ (a) Identify the type of rainfall indicated in the diagram.

____

(b) Explain how this type of rainfall occurs.

____

____

(c) Why might precipitation be higher at X than at Y?

____

____

5 Link each term in column 1 with its matching pair in column 2.

Column 1		Column 2	
A	Relief rainfall		Associated with summer in inland areas.
B	Cyclonic rainfall		Most common form of precipitation.
C	Convectional rainfall		Also called frontal rainfall.
D	Rainfall		Associated with upland or mountainous areas.

4.7 Weather

1 Link each term in column 1 with its matching pair in column 2. One match has been made for you.

Column 1		Column 2	
A	Meteorology		Much information about weather is gathered here.
B	Met Éireann		The study of weather.
C	Weather station		The state of the atmosphere at any moment in time.
D	Weather		Ireland's Weather Centre.
E	Open, low ground	E	Ideal location for a weather station.

2 Link each term in column 1 with its matching pair in column 2.

Column 1		Column 2	
A	Stevenson's screen		Box where some weather instruments are stored.
B	Meteorology		Where weather recording instruments are located.
C	Weather station		Can be made after the gathering and analysis of weather data.
D	Weather forecast		The study of weather.

3 Identify each weather instrument shown below.

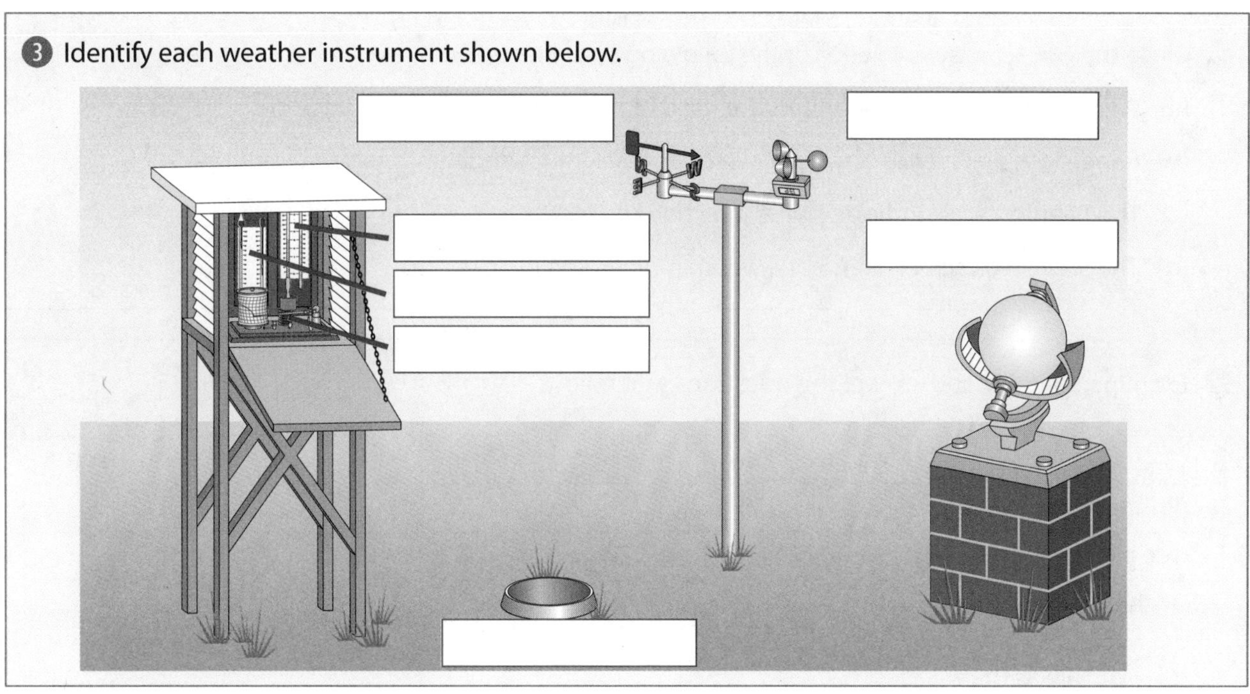

4 Complete the following table about weather instruments.

Instrument	What it measures	Unit of measurement
Thermometer		
	Precipitation	
Barometer		
		km/hr or mph
	Sunshine	

5 Explain each of the following terms.

(a) Isotherm:

___

___

(b) Isobars:

___

___

(c) Degrees Celsius:

___

___

(d) Beaufort scale:

___

___

6 Circle the correct answer in each of the following statements:

(a) Wet and dry bulb thermometers are used to measure *humidity / temperature*.

(b) Range is the *difference between / average of* maximum and minimum temperature.

(c) The Beaufort scale indicates wind *direction / strength*.

(d) The Stevenson screen *is / is not* a weather recording instrument.

7 Examine the table and answer the questions that follow.

	Mon	Tue	Wed	Thu	Fri	Sat	Sun
Temperature (°C)	10	12	17	8	11	9	10
Precipitation (mm)	9	6	0	13	2	1	5
Sunshine (hrs / day)	3	3	7	1	5	4	3

(a) Which was the warmest day? ____________________

(b) Which was the coldest day? ____________________

(c) What is the temperature range? ____________________

(d) What is the average daily temperature? ____________________

(e) How many dry days were there? ____________________

(f) What was the total precipitation for the week? ____________________

(g) What was the total sunshine for the week? ____________________

(h) Why, do you think, was there so little sunshine on Thursday? ____________________

8 Examine the table and answer the questions that follow.

Month	J	F	M	A	M	J	J	A	S	O	N	D
Temperature (°C)	24	26	26	27	27	26	28	28	26	27	25	24
Precipitation (mm)	305	357	357	320	260	170	150	109	90	85	68	149

(a) The annual range of temperature is *4°C / 26°C*.

(b) The total precipitation for the two coldest months is *156 mm / 454 mm*.

(c) The mean temperature for June, July, and August is *2°C / 27°C*.

(d) The wettest season is *spring / winter*.

(e) The warmest season is *summer / autumn*.

9 Select any one weather instrument and answer the following.

Name of instrument: ____________________

What it measures: ____________________

Unit of measurement: ____________________

4.8 The greenhouse effect and global warming

1 Circle the correct answer in each of the following statements:

(a) The greenhouse effect *is a natural process / results from human activity.*

(b) Global warming *is a natural process / results from human activity.*

(c) Greenhouse gases include *methane and carbon dioxide / oxygen and nitrogen.*

(d) Fossil fuels include *HEP and solar energy / coal and oil.*

(e) Global warming will lead to an *increase / decrease* in sea levels.

2 List three activities that contribute to global warming.

(a) ____________________

(b) ____________________

(c) ____________________

3 Complete the flow chart to explain global warming using the terms below.

the atmosphere becomes warmer

gases are released into the atmosphere

lowlands are flooded and drought occurs

global temperatures increase

more solar heat is trapped

ice-caps melt and evaporation increases

START Forests cut down and fossil fuels burned →

FINISH

4 Describe two possible negative effects of global warming.

(a) ____________________

(b) ____________________

5 Suggest some ways by which global warming could be reduced.

(a) ____________________

(b) ____________________

Revision crossword

Down

2 Rainfall associated with hilly regions
3 The wind that is most frequent in an area
5 Large bodies of air with different temperature and pressure (3, 6)
6 The Labrador and Canaries are .... currents
8 Pressure created when air is cooled and descends
10 Also known as the hydrologic cycle (5, 5)
11 Gas that makes up most of the atmosphere
13 Lines joining places of equal pressure
15 A cold air mass from the north

Across

1 The state of the atmosphere at a particular time and place
4 The North Atlantic Drift begins as this (4, 6)
7 The layer of the atmosphere that protects us from UV rays
9 Moving air
12 Effect where winds are deflected as the Earth spins on its axis
14 Difference between maximum and minimum temperatures
16 Heat and light from the sun (5, 6)
17 Angular distance north or south of the equator

CHAPTER 5

CLIMATES AND NATURAL REGIONS

5.1 Introducing climate

1 Weather and climate

(a) What is meant by the term 'climate'?

Climate is the average contion of the weather over a long period of time

(b) List two differences between weather and climate.

(i) ______

(ii) ______

2 Explain how the following factors influence world climate.

(a) Latitude:

The angular distance north or south of the equator.

(b) Distance from the sea:

~~is precipitation that an area reci~~

(c) Prevailing wind:

is precipitation that an area recieves.

3 Answer the following questions on local climate.

(a) What is meant by the term 'local climate'?

The climate experienced by a small region

(b) List two factors that influence local climate.

(i) ~~Aspect~~ Altitude the height above sea level

(ii) Aspect ~~Altitude~~ the direction a slope face in relation to the sun rais

4 Explain why it is much colder at B than at A.

B is more exposed to wind and receive more precipitation.

5 Examine the diagram and answer the following questions.

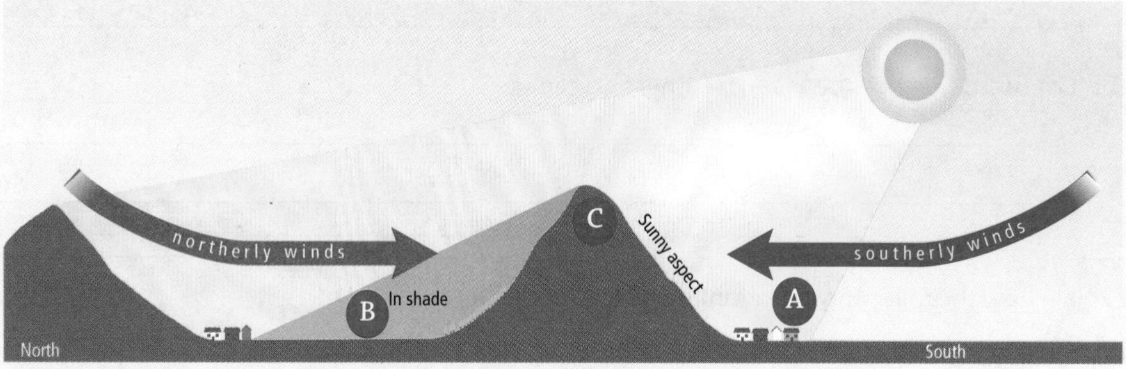

(a) List two advantages of living at A.

(i) Get warm wind

(ii) furter away from mued slope

(b) List two disadvantages of living at B.

(i) Cold winds

(ii)

(c) Why would very few people choose to live at C?

5.2 Natural regions and world climates

1 Natural regions

(a) What is meant by the term natural region?

An area of the world that has own unique characteristics.

(b) List four characteristics that help define a natural region.

(i) Climate

(ii) Wildlife

(iii) Natural Vegetation

(iv) Human activities

2 (a) What is meant by the term 'natural vegetation'?

____

____

(b) How might a region be influenced by its climate?

____

____

3 Broad climate zones

Examine the diagram below and answer the following questions.

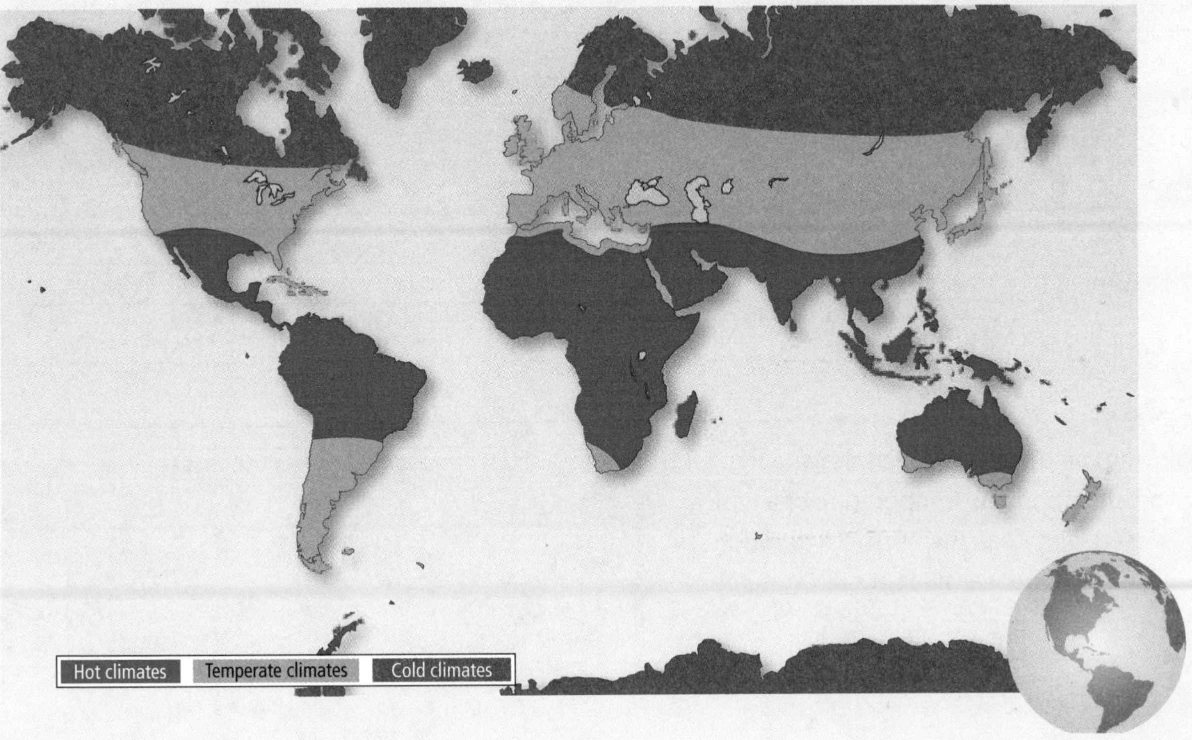

(a) Name a continent that does not have a hot climate. ________________

(b) Name a continent that does not have a cold climate. Spain

(c) Which continent has the greatest area affected by hot climate? Africa

(d) Name a continent that has hot, temperate and cold climates. ________________

5.3 Hot climates of the world

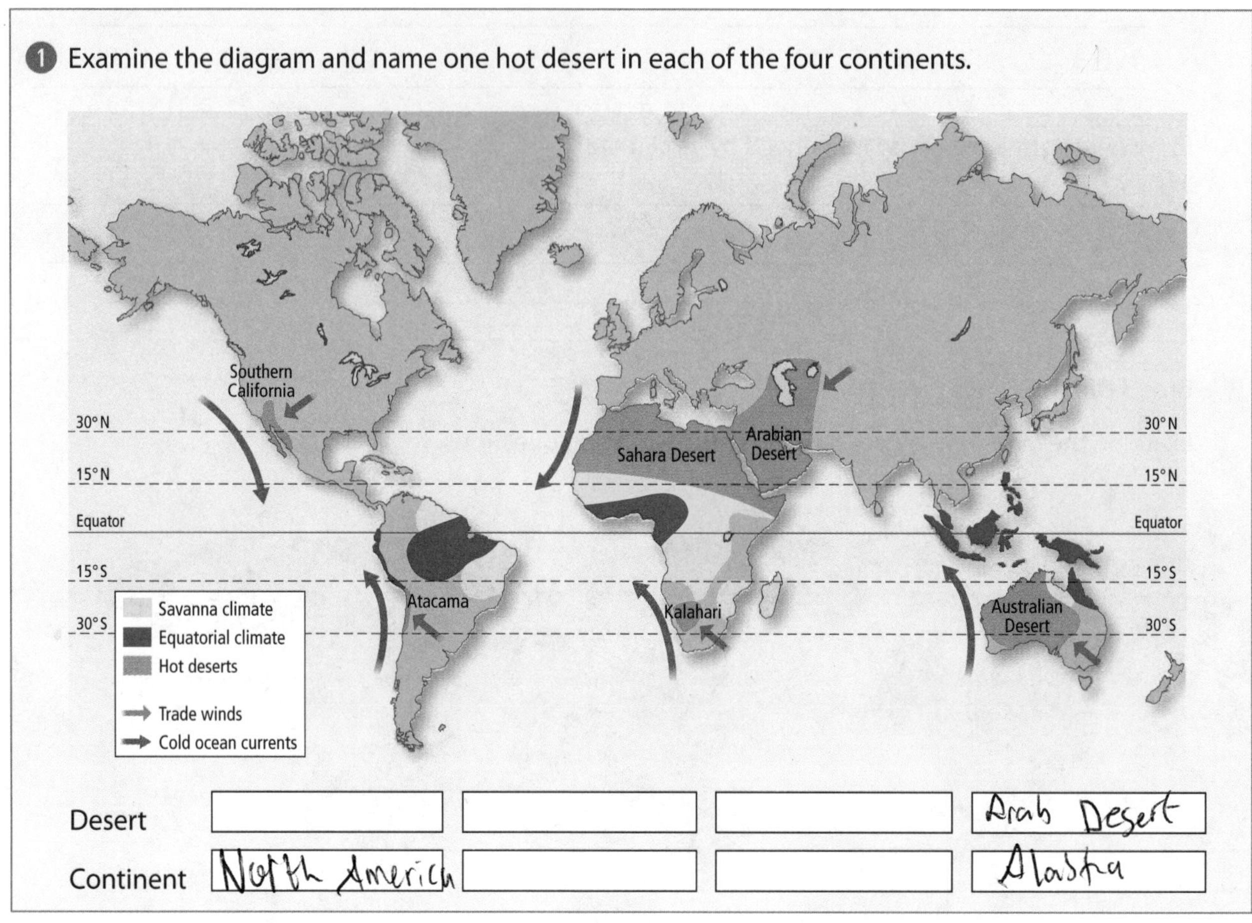

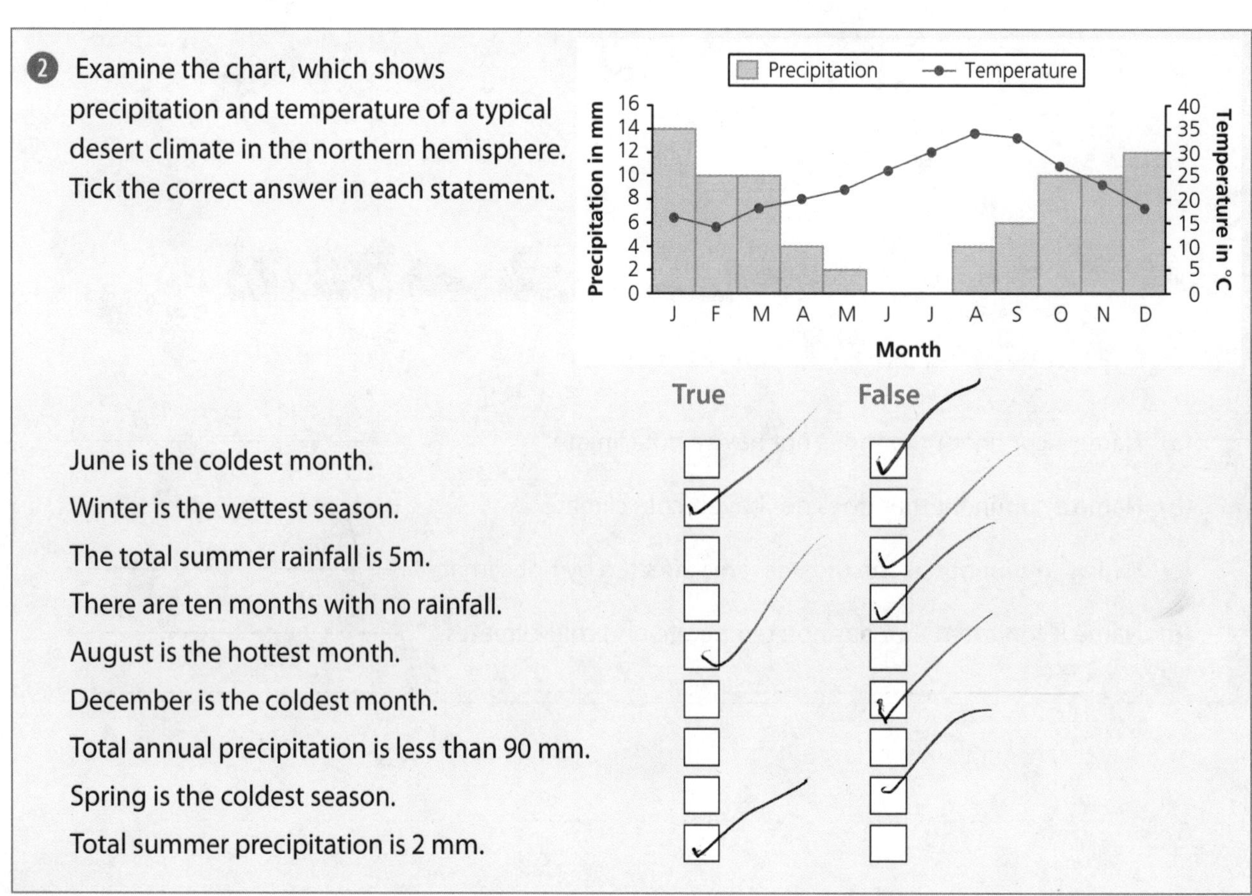

3 Complete the grid below to explain hot desert climate.

Characteristic	Reason
High daytime temperatures	in the tropics. Sun is always high
Low night-time temperatures	The hot deserts are in the path of the trade winds
Very low amounts of precipitation	These blow overland towards the equator

4 Describe three ways in which plants have adapted in order to survive in a desert climate.

(a) Shallow roots

(b) Spikes

(c) Tick wax

26 JAN 2017

5 Link each term in column 1 with its matching pair in column 2.

Column 1	
A	Oasis
B	Cactus
C	Camel
D	Taproot

Column 2	
D	Allows plants to get water from deep underground.
B	Animal known as the 'ship of the desert'.
C	Desert plant with waxy skin and needles.
A	Where water is found close to the surface in a desert.

6 **The Sahel**

(a) What is the Sahel?

Sahel is the Southern area of the Sahara

(b) Name any three countries that make up part of the Sahel.

(i) Mali (ii) Niger (ii) Senegal

7 Desertification

(a) Explain the term desertification.

It means turning land into desert.

(b) Explain how climate change has led to desertification.

There is not much rain there is higher temperatures and rivers have dried up

(c) Explain how population growth has led to desertification.

It has led to desertification because there is a high demand for food

8 Describe any two results of desertification.

(a) people leave

(b) people migrate.

9 List two ways by which desertification might be reduced.

(a) Slow down soil

(b) Dig deeper wells

5.4 Temperate climates of the world

1 (a) Name two temperate climates.

(i) Cold temperatures

(ii) warm temperatures

(b) Which temperate climate does Ireland experience?

Rain and cold wind

(c) What is the natural vegetation of Ireland?

Cold

(d) Why was it removed?

2 Complete the grid below to explain hot desert climate.

Factor	Description
Summer temperatures	
Winter temperatures	
Precipitation	

3 **Warm temperate oceanic climate**

(a) Give another name for warm temperate oceanic climate. ______________________

(b) Between what latitude is warm temperate oceanic climate found? ________________

(c) Name four European countries that experience this climate.

(i) ______________________ (ii) ______________________

(iii) ______________________ (iv) ______________________

4 Circle the correct answers in each statement:

(a) Mediterranean climate is found in countries such as *Italy and Spain / Norway and Sweden* between latitudes *30° and 40° / 40° and 50°* north and south of the equator.

(b) Mediterranean summers are *hot and dry / warm and moist* because of *clear skies and sunshine / cloudy skies and rain-bearing winds.*

(c) Mediterranean winters are *cold and wet / mild and moist* because the *prevailing wind is warm and the sun is fairly high in the sky / winds are cold and latitude is high.*

(d) The natural vegetation of the Mediterranean region was *grassland / evergreen woodland* which was removed as a result of *forest fires / clearing land for agriculture.*

(e) Today, the natural vegetation consists of *ferns and grasses / shrubs and herbs*, including *lavender and thyme / gorse and ferns.*

5 Circle the correct answers in each statement:

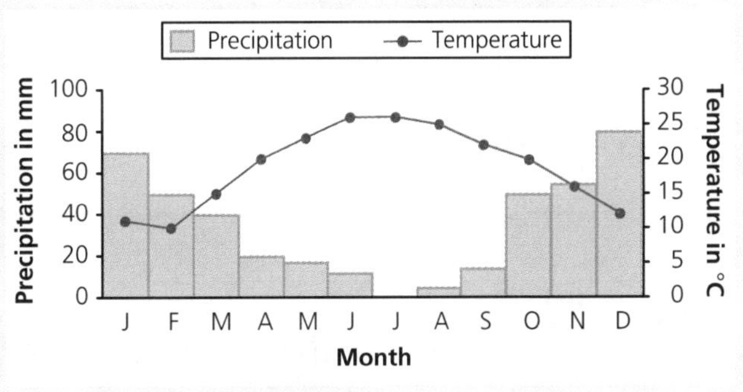

(a) The driest month is *July / August.*

(b) The hottest month is *June / August.*

(c) The wettest month is *December / January.*

(d) The coldest month is *January / February.*

(e) The average temperature for November is *15°C / 17°C.*

(f) The total rainfall for May, June and July is *20 mm / 35 mm.*

(g) Temperatures between June and August are higher than *25°C / 28°C.*

(h) The annual temperature range is *10°C / 17°C.*

6 The Mediterranean region

(a) List two ways by which the natural vegetation in a Mediterranean area has adapted to its environment.

(i) ____________________

____

(ii) ____________________

____

(b) How has agriculture damaged the vegetation and soil in Mediterranean regions?

____

____

(c) Name three citrus fruits grown in Mediterranean regions.

(i) ____________________

(ii) ____________________

(iii) ____________________

(d) How are these crops suited to a Mediterranean climate?

____

____

____

____

7 Irrigation

(a) Explain the term irrigation.

____

____

____

(b) Why is irrigation important for agriculture?

____

____

____

(c) Name two crops grown with the aid of irrigation.

(i) ____________________

(ii) ____________________

8 With the aid of your atlas, identify the tourism destinations marked A to H in the map below.

Mediterranean Sea

Mediterranean climate

A ____________ B Benidorm C Barcelona

D Venice E Athens F Greece

G Egypt H Tunisia

9 Select any one of the resorts named in question 8 and explain two reasons why you would like to holiday there.

Resort name: Egypt

(a) To see the Phrimids

(b) To play in the sand.

5.5 Cold climates of the world

1 (a) What does the term boreal mean?

Boreal means Nothern

(b) Between what latitudes is the boreal climate found?

55°N and Artic Circle

(c) Name two countries that experience boreal climate.

(i) Canada

(ii) Alaska

2 Complete each of the following statements:

(a) Summers in boreal regions are cool and short because

(b) Winters in boreal regions are cold and long because

(c) Annual precipitation in boreal regions is low because

3 Examine the chart and circle the correct answers in the statements below.

Month	J	F	M	A	M	J	J	A	S	O	N	D
Temperature (°C)	-30	-25	-20	-17	-7	2	3	2	-2	-7	-18	-28
Precipitation (mm)	10	15	10	15	15	16	25	25	16	25	10	15

(a) The coldest month is *January / July*.

(b) The average temperature for August and September is *2°C / 0°C*

(c) The temperature range is *33°C / 27°C*.

(d) The wettest season is *winter / autumn*.

(e) Temperatures are below freezing point for *9 / 3* months of the year.

4 Complete the temperature graph, using the information in the chart in question 3 above.

5 (a) Give another name for the evergreen forest of the boreal region.

(b) What type of trees grow in the taiga?

(c) How have these trees adapted to their environment?

(d) Why do the trees grow so slowly?

(i)

(ii)

6 Examine the diagram on the right. Insert the correct letter in each box and fill in the blank spaces.

[B] Permafrost is ground that is permanently hard

[A] Shallow roots grow out due to permafrost.

[D] Needles means there is less moisture

[E] Branches grow downwards so that snow slides off.

[C] A thick bark helps the tree to retain moisture.

7 Identify two animals or birds that live in the boreal region and describe how each has adapted to that environment.

Animal/bird	How it has adapted to its environment
1 Bear	hibernating, migrating
2 Wolf	Growin thick fur

8 People and economy of the boreal region

(a) Why do so few people live in the boreal region?

(i) The harsh climate

(ii) few towns.

(b) How has the lifestyle of the Sami people changed over recent times?

(c) Why is the boreal forest an important economic resource?

Its important because theres a lot of animals who live their

Revision crossword

Down

1 The spread of desert conditions
2 Animal known as the 'ship of the desert'
3 The region at the southern edge of the Sahara Desert
6 Desert plant with waxy skin, needles and spreading roots
9 The evergreen forest of the boreal region
10 Trees that are cone-bearing
11 What bears do during the long cold winter
13 Difference between highest and lowest temperatures
15 Long period without any precipitation
17 Along with altitude, this influences local climates

Across

4 Fertile area in a desert where water is close to the surface
5 Large desert in North Africa
7 Climate belt found to the south of the Arctic Circle
8 Climates found in the mid-latitudes
12 Important economic activity in regions with a Mediterranean climate
14 Climates found close to the poles are .... climates
16 A tribal people who live in Mali
18 Forest type native to regions with cool temperate oceanic climate
19 What happens to soil as a result of drought and deforestation
20 Distance north or south of the equator that influences climate
21 Climates found close to the equator are .... climates

CHAPTER 6

SOILS

6.1 What is soil?

1 (a) Examine the diagram howing the make-up of a typical soil sample. List the elements that make up the sample in decreasing order of volume.

(i) Air

(ii) Living orgars

(iii) Water

(iv) Humus

(v) Mineral matter

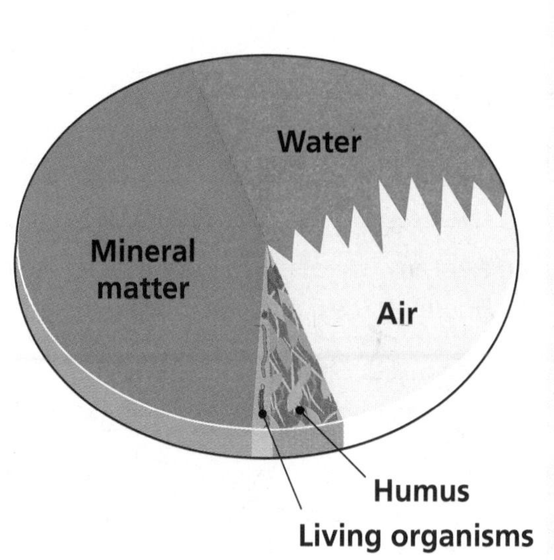

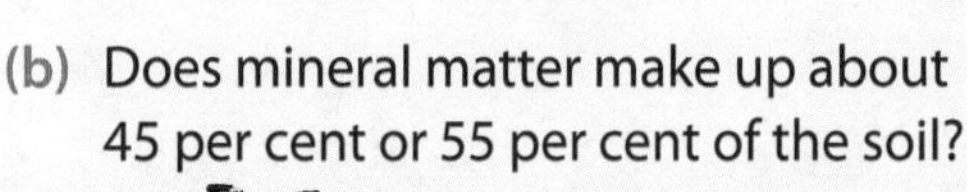

(b) Does mineral matter make up about 45 per cent or 55 per cent of the soil?

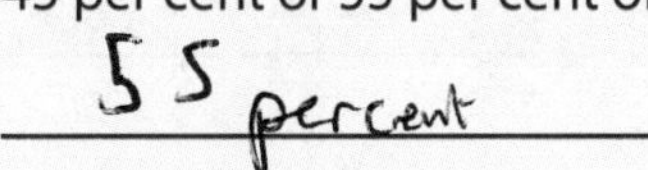

55 percent

2 In the boxes provided, link each description in column 1 with its pair in column 2.

A	Humus
B	Micro-organisms
C	Air
D	Mineral matter
E	Water

	Broken-down rock particles.
	Contains dissolved minerals.
	Small creatures in the soil.
	Plant and animals remains.
C	Contains oxygen for root growth.

3 Insert the following words in the appropriate blank spaces in the diagram below.

soil time humus minerals rocks vegetation

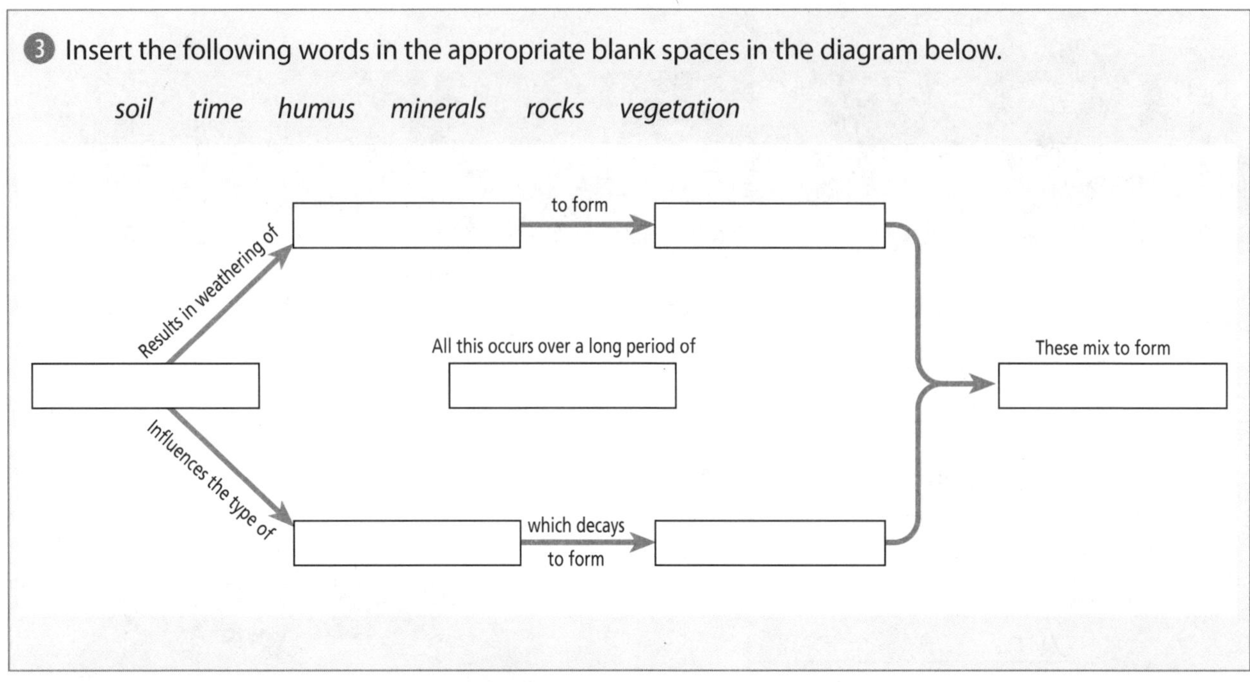

4 Select any two of the following factors and explain the part of each in soil formation:

climate parent material vegetation living organisms landscape ~~time~~

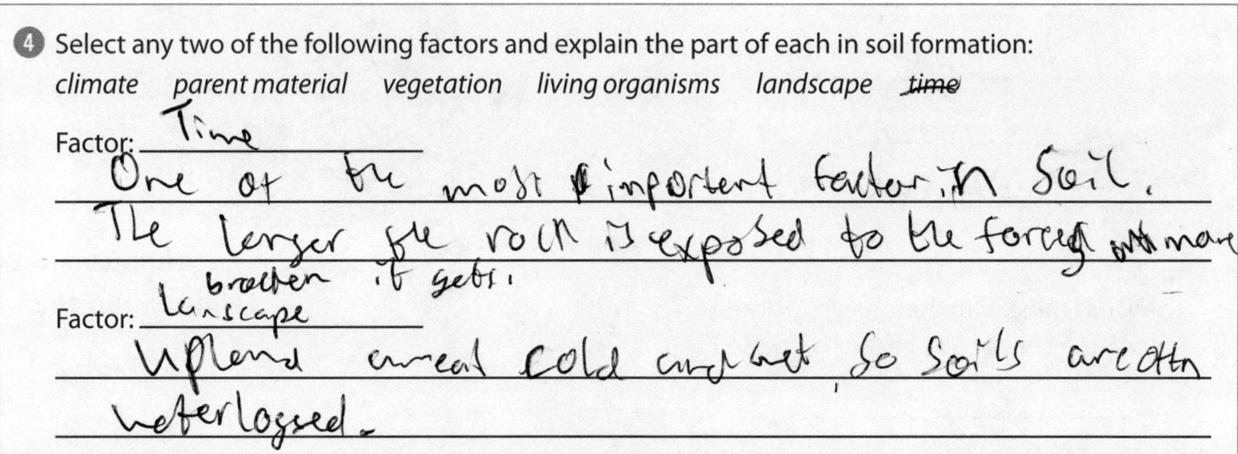

Factor: Time

One of the most important factor in Soil. The larger the rock is exposed to the forces the more broken it gets.

Factor: Landscape

Upland area cold and wet, so Soils are often waterlogged.

5 Link each term with its correct number on the diagram.

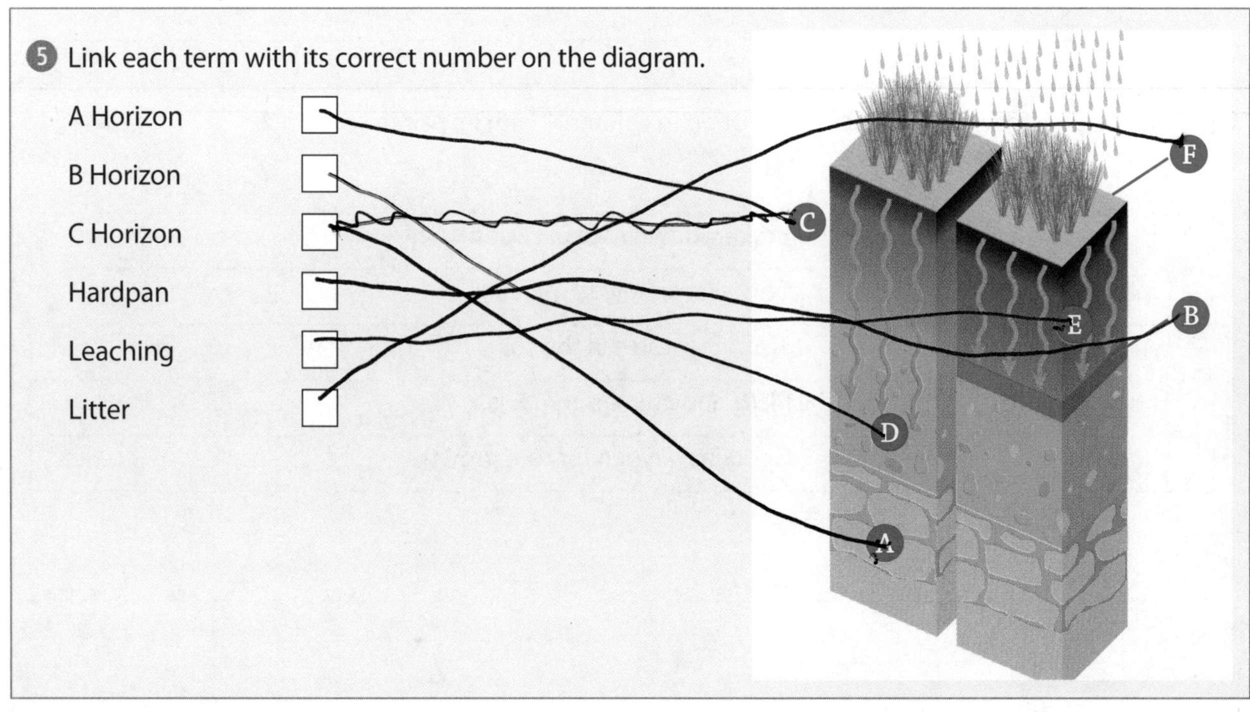

6 Link each term in column 1 with its matching pair in column 2.

	Column 1		Column 2
A	Humus		Different layers of soil.
B	Leaching	E	Influences the formation of soil.
C	Hardpan		Washes minerals into lower horizons.
D	Soil profile		Provides nutrients for the soil.
E	Climate		Layer of hard material at bottom of A horizon.

7 Circle the correct answer in each of the following statements:

(a) The amount of *water / humus* in soil varies between winter and summer.

(b) The micro-organisms in soil include *worms / grass* and *slugs / clay*.

(c) Mineral matter in soil includes *clay / insects* and *oxygen / sand*.

(d) Leaching can result in *well-drained / badly-drained* soil.

8 Select the odd-one-out.

(a) water, air, hardpan hardpan

(b) soil profile, leaching, hardpan Soil profile

(c) time, parent rock, vegetation parent rock

6.2 Irish soils

1 Examine the map showing the soils of Ireland and answer the following questions.

(a) What is the most common soil type found in Ireland?

~~Podzol Soil~~ Brown earth Soil

(b) Identify each of the following soil types and name any one county where it is found.

Brown earth soils
Peaty soils
Podzol soils
Gley soils

	Soil type	County
A	Peaty Soil	Cork / Kerry / Galway / Leitrim / Donegal
B	Grey Soils	Clare / Down / Tyrone / Fermanagh
C	Podzols Soil	places around Ireland
D	Brown earth Soil	Rest of Ireland

(c) What is the main soil type in your county?

Brown earth Soil

2 Link each term in column 1 with its matching pair in column 2.

	Column 1
A	Brown soil
B	Peaty soil
C	Podzol soil
D	Tropical red soil

	Column 2
B	Associated with wet, cold, upland areas.
D	Not found in Ireland.
A	Most common soil type in Ireland.
C	Usually found in areas of coniferous forest.

3 Choose two Irish soils and describe any three differences between them.

	Soil type 1 Brown earth soils	Soil type 2 Podzol Soils
Difference 1	Main Soil in Ireland	Covered by Coniferous forests.
Difference 2	found in South, Midland and east	Small amounts of humus
Difference 3	Very little leaching	Upland areas Cork, Galway and Tipperary

4 Explain two ways in which soil is important to humans.

(a) So humans can grow Vegtabilles and to grow grass for cows to eat to get milk.

(b) To grow crops like wheat for cearials.

6.3 Tropical red soils

1 Fill in the blanks using the words below.

climate rainfall ~~red rust~~ ~~temperatures weathering~~ leaching

The single biggest influence on the formation of tropical red soils is *weathering*. The high *temperatures* and plentiful ~~[illegible]~~ *rainfall* encourage *leaching* and so these soils are very deep. Iron in the soil is broken down into iron oxide or *rust*, giving the soil its *red* colour. The heavy rainfall also leads to ~~[illegible]~~ *climate* of minerals.

2 Explain how tropical red soils quickly lose their fertility.

6.4 Natural vegetation and soil

1 Describe two ways in which soil can influence the vegetation of an area.

(a)

(b)

2 Describe two ways in which vegetation can influence the soil of an area.

(a)

(b)

Revision crossword

Down

1 This fills the pore spaces in soil
2 These soils develop on impermeable rock or clay
3 Surface layer of plant material
5 When soil is removed by wind or rain
7 Soil type in boggy, upland areas
8 Soil that developed beneath coniferous forests
9 Soil takes a lot of this to form
10 Washing nutrients downwards in soil
11 Another name for the B Horizon
12 Found at the bottom of the B horizon
15 ______pan creates an impermeable layer in the soil

Across

4 This matter consists of the remains of rocks
6 Brown soil
9 Red soils are found in this climatic region
13 Common name for iron oxide
14 This contains dissolved minerals
16 A or B or C
17 Colour of the most common soil in Ireland
18 Fine material that is easily waterlogged

Chapter 7

Maps and Photographs

Legend
Eochair

Ordnance Survey Ireland — Suirbhéireacht Ordanáis Éireann — DISCOVERY SERIES — SRAITH EOLAIS

Eolas Turasóireachta / Tourist Information

- Láithreán carbhán (idirthurais) / Caravan site (transit)
- Brú de chuid An Óige / Youth Hostel (An Óige)
- Brú saoire Neamhspleách / Independent Holiday Hostel
- Ionad pairceála / Parking
- Láithreán picnicí / Picnic site
- Teileafón Poiblí / Public Telephone
- Láithreán campála / Camping site
- Ionad eolais turasóireachta (ar oscailt ar feadh na bliana) / Tourist Information centre (regular opening)
- Ionad eolais turasóireachta (ar oscailt le linn an tséasúir) / Tourist Information centre (restricted opening)
- Ionad dearctha / Viewpoint
- An Taisce / National Trust
- Tearmann Dúlra / Nature Reserve
- Galfchúrsa, machaire gailf / Golf Course or Links

Bóithre / Roads

- M 1 — Mótarbhealach / Motorway (Junction number)
- N 11 — Bóthar príomha náisiúnta / National Primary Road
- N 71 — Bóthar tánaisteach náisiúnta / National Secondary Road
- Carrbhealach dúbailte / Dual Carriageway
- Bóthar príomha /tánaisteach náisiúnta beartaithe / Proposed Nat. Primary / Secondary Road
- R 574 — Bóthar Réigiúnach / Regional Road
- Bóthar den tríú grád / Third Class Road (4 metres min / 4 metres max)
- Bóithre de chineál eile / Other Roads
- Bealach / Track

Teorainneacha / Boundaries

- Teorainn idirnáisiúnta / International Boundary
- Teorainn chontae / County Boundary
- Páirc Náisiúnta / National Park
- Páirc Foraoise / Forest Park
- Seilbh de chuid an Aire Chosanta / Dept. of Defence Property
- Foraois bhuaircíneach / Coniferous Plantation
- Coill nádúrtha / Natural Woodland
- Foraois mheasctha / Mixed Woodland

Gnéithe ginearálta / General features

- Foirgnimh le hais a chéile / Built up Area
- Aerfort / Airport
- Aerpháirc / Airfield
- Oifig phoist / Post office
- Garda Síochána / Police
- Stáisiún cumhachta (uisce) / Power Station (Hydro)
- Stáisiún cumhachta (breosla iontaiseach) / Power Station (Fossil)
- Líne tarchurtha leictreachais / Electricity Transmission Line
- Crann / Mast
- Eaglais no séipéal / Church or Chapel
- Ardeaglais / Cathedral
- Cuaille triantánachta / Triangulation Pillar
- Trasnú cliathráin / Graticule Intersection
- Siúlbhealach le comharthaí; gan comharthaí / Waymarked Walks; Unmarked
- Ferry V — Bád fartha (feithiclí) / Ferry (Vehicle)
- Ferry P — Bád fartha (paisinéirí) / Ferry (Passenger)

Séadchomhartha / Antiquities

- Séadchomhartha Ainmnithe / Named Antiquities
- Clós, m.sh. Ráth nó Lios / Enclosure, e.g. Ringfort
- Láthair Chatha (le dáta) / Battlefield (with date)

Relif / Relief

- Céim imlíne comhairde 10m / 10m Contour Interval
- Céim imlíne comhairde 50m / 50m Contour Interval
- 123 • Spota airde / Spot Height

Gnéithe uisce / Water features

- Loch / Lake
- Canáil, canáil (thirim) / Canal, Canal (dry)
- Abhainn nó sruthán / River or Stream
- Teach Solais in úsáid / as úsáid / Lighthouse in use / disuse
- Bádóireacht / Boating activities
- Líne bharr láin / High Water Mark
- Líne lag trá / Low Water Mark (shingle, mud sand or loose rock)
- Trá / Beach

Compiled and published by Ordnance Survey Ireland, Phoenix Park, Dublin 8, Ireland.
Arna thiomsú agus arna fhoilsiú ag Shuirbhéireacht Ordanáis Éireann, Páirc an Fhionnuisce, Baile Átha Cliath 8, Éire.

Iarnróid / Railways

- Iarnróid / Railways
- Iarnród tionscalaíoch / Industrial Line
- Tollán / Tunnel
- LC — Crosaire comhréidh / Level Crossing
- Staisiún traenach / Railway Station

IRISH NATIONAL GRID

A	B	C	D	E
F	G	H	J	K
L	M	N	O	P
Q	R	S	T	U
V	W	X	Y	Z

Unauthorised reproduction infringes Ordnance Survey Ireland and Government of Ireland copyright. All rights reserved. No part of this publication may be copied, reproduced or transmitted in any form or by any means without the prior written permission of the copyright owners.

Séraíonn atáirgeadh neamhúdaraithe cóipcheart Shuirbhéireacht Ordanáis Éireann agus Rialtas na hÉireann. Gach ceart ar cosnamh. Ní ceadmhach aon chuid den fhoilseachán seo a chóipeáil, a atáirgeadh nó a tharchur in aon fhoirm ná ar aon bhealach gan cead i scríbhinn roimh ré ó úinéirí an chóipchirt.

SCALE 1:50 000
SCÁLA 1:50 000

KILOMETRES: 1 0 1 2 3 4 5 6 7 8
STATUTE MILES: 1 0 1 2 3 4 5

2 ceintiméadar sa chiliméadar (taobh chearnóg eangaí) 2 centimetres to 1 Kilometre (grid square side)

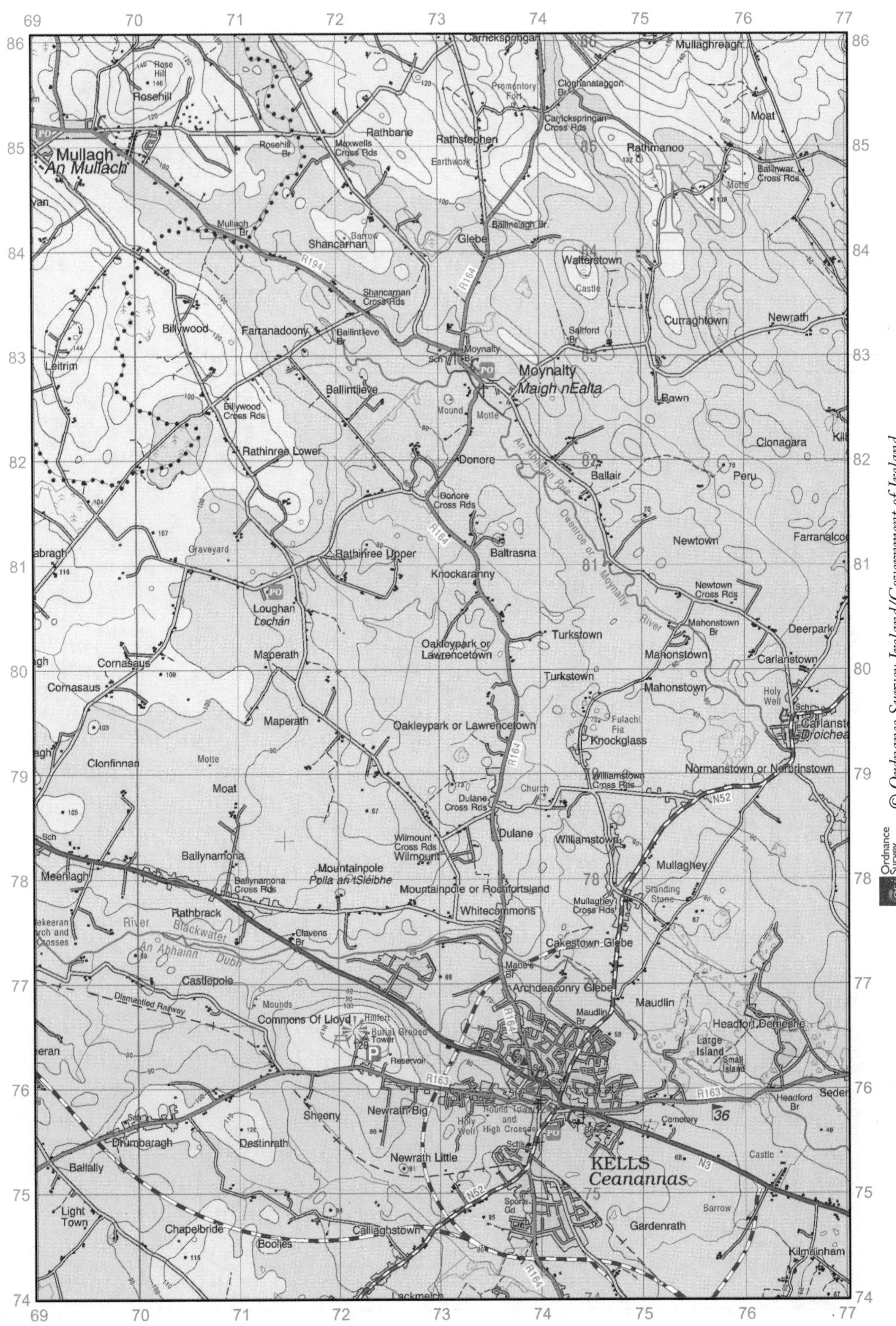

© Ordnance Survey Ireland/Government of Ireland
Ordnance Survey Ireland OSi

Kells

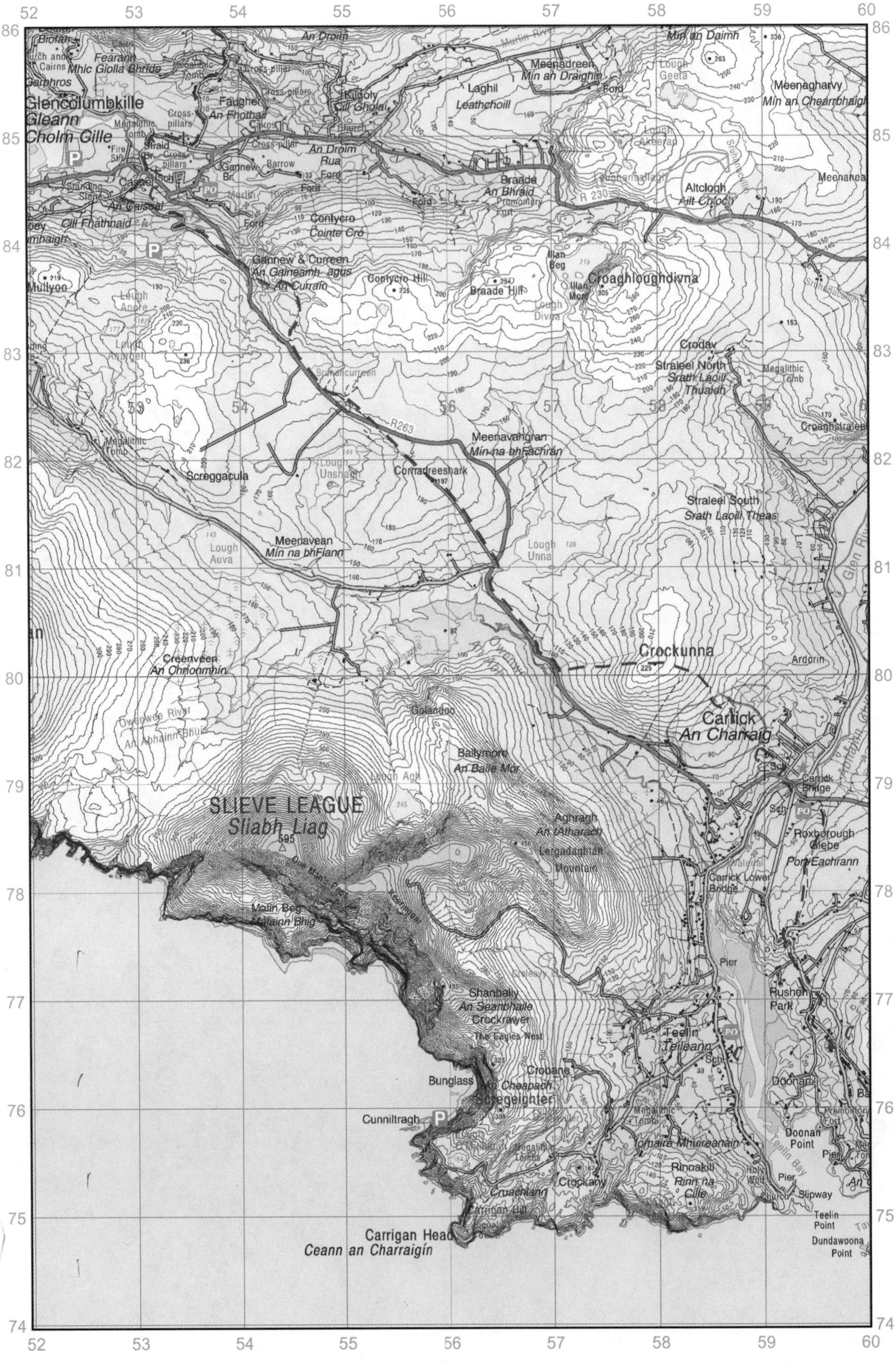

© Ordnance Survey Ireland/Government of Ireland

Clonakilty

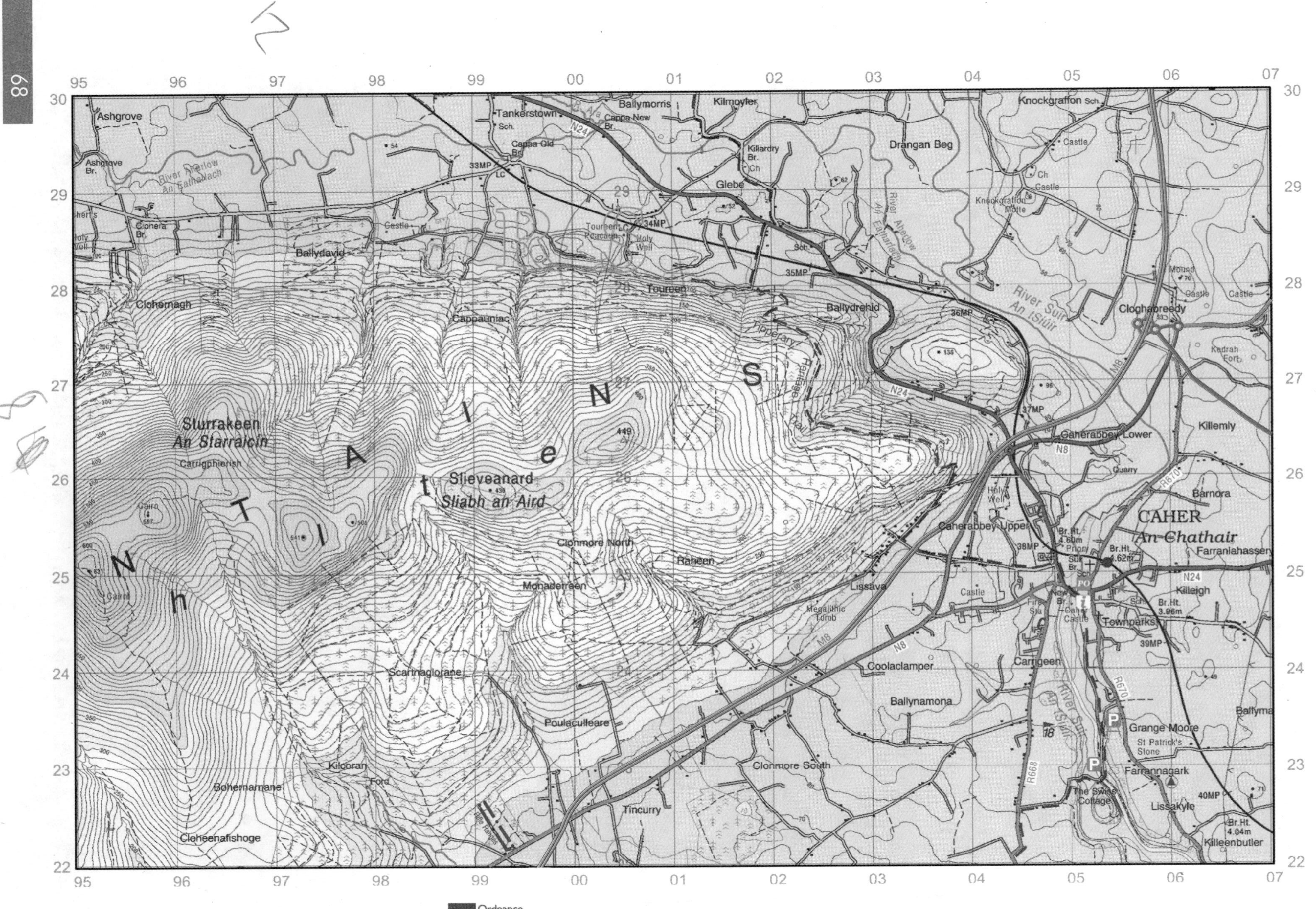

© Ordnance Survey Ireland/Government of Ireland

Caher

© Ordnance Survey Ireland/Government of Ireland

Timoleague

7.1 Ordnance Survey maps

Map legend

1 The map legend on page 63 shows the symbols used in the Ordnance Survey maps. Draw the symbol used to show each of the following:

(a) Post Office		(b) Viewpoint	
(c) Caravan Site		(d) Picnic Site	
(e) Youth Hostel		(f) Golf Course	
(g) Parking		(h) Tourist Information Centre	
(i) Antiquities		(j) Garda Siochána	

Scale and measuring distance

2 List the three methods of showing scale on an Ordnance Survey map.

(a) ____________ (b) ____________ (c) ____________

3 The OS Discovery Series of maps is drawn to a scale of 1:50,000, where 2 cm on a map represents 1 km on the ground. Using this scale, calculate the distance in kilometres represented by each of these lines.

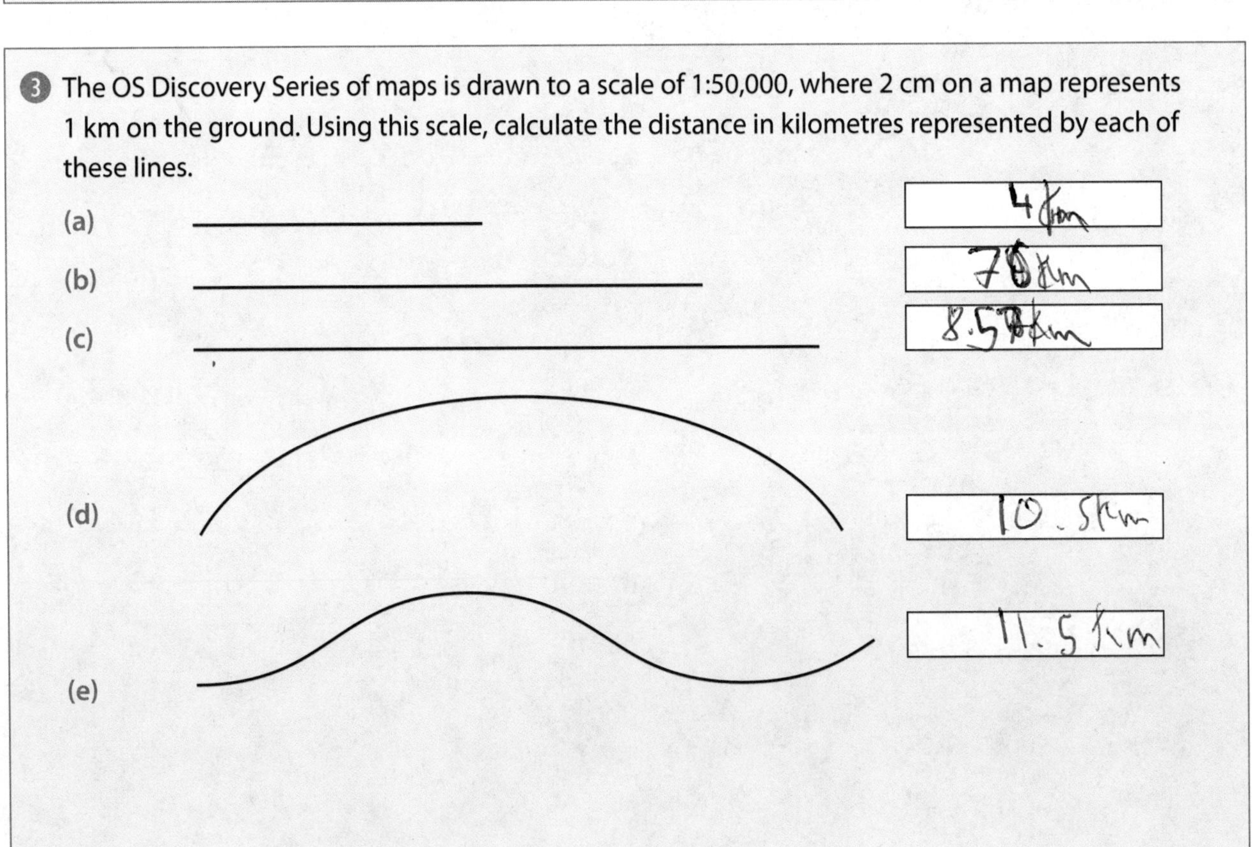

4 Refer to the Kells map on page 64 and calculate each of the following straight-line distances. Give your answer in kilometres.

(a) Post Office at Moynalty to Post Office at Mullagh. 4.5 Km

(b) Public Telephone at Carlanstown to Post Office at Kells. 4.5km

(c) Post Office at Moynalty to Post Office at Kells. 7.25km

5 Refer to the Kells map on page 64 and calculate each of the following distances, giving your answers in kilometres.

(a) The distance along the R194 from the Post Office at Mullagh to the Post Office at Moynalty.

17

(b) The distance along the N52 from the Public Telephone at Carlanstown to the junction with the N3.

______

6 Refer to the Glencolumbkille map on page 66.

(a) Calculate the area of the map extract in km^2. 96

(b) Calculate the area of open sea in km^2. 13

Grid references

7 Examine the grid and give a four-figure grid reference for each letter marked.

A ______

B ______

C ______

D ______

E ______

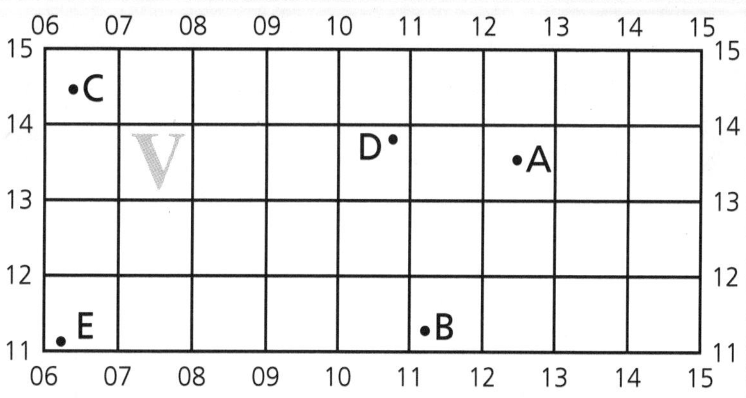

8 Examine the grid and give a four-figure grid reference for each letter marked.

U ____________

V ____________

W ____________

X ____________

Y ____________

Z ____________

9 Refer to the Caher map extract on page 68 and give a four-figure grid reference for each of the following:

(a) Rifle Range ____________ (b) Golf Course ____________

(c) Railway Station ____________ (d) Slieveanard ____________

(e) Picnic Site ____________ (f) Youth Hostel ____________

10 Refer to the Timoleague map on page 70 and identify the antiquity at each of the following four-figure grid references.

(a) W 46 41 ____________ (b) W 45 37 ____________

(c) W 51 44 ____________ (d) W 47 39 ____________

(e) W 50 35 ____________ (f) W 52 44 ____________

11 Refer to the Kells map extract on page 64 and give a six-figure grid reference for each of the following.

(a) Parking ____________ (b) Moynalty PO ____________

(c) Kells Post Office ____________ (d) Youth Hostel ____________

(e) Golf Course ____________ (f) Holy Well ____________

12 Refer to the Caher map on page 68 and identify the antiquity at each of the following six-figure grid references.

(a) R 982 286 ____________ (b) S 062 278 ____________

(c) R 957 256 ____________ (d) S 039 250 ____________

(e) S 024 247 ____________ (f) S 006 284 ____________

13 Refer to the Glencolumbkille map extract on page 66. Link each feature in column 1 with its grid reference in column 2.

	Column 1
A	Post Office
B	Garda Station
C	Megalith Tomb
D	Lake
E	Mountain top
F	Parking
G	School
H	Viewpoint

	Column 2
	G 592 788
	G 550 820
	G 592 787
	G 525 848
	G 589 827
	G 537 845
	G 544 785
	G 594 791

14 Identify the directions lettered A to F on the diagram below.

A East

B South

C North

D South east

E South east

F North West

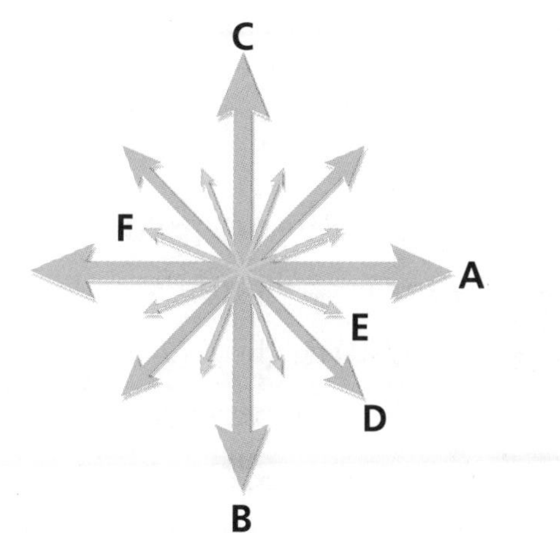

15 Refer to the Glencolumbkille map on page 66 and circle the correct direction in each statement.

(a) Carrick (G 590 790) lies to the *south east / north west* of Glencolumbkille (G 530 845).

(b) Lough Auva (G 538 812) lies to the *west / east* of Lough Unna (G 570 812).

(c) Slieve League (G 544 784) lies to the *south / north* of Meenavean (G 545 812).

(d) The Owenwee river flows into the sea in a *south-easterly / south-westerly* direction.

Height

16 Identify the four methods by which height is represented on an Ordnance Survey map.

(a) Colour (b) Contones (c) Spot hieght (d) Trangulat top pillars

⑰ Examine the diagram and estimate the height of each of the locations marked on it.

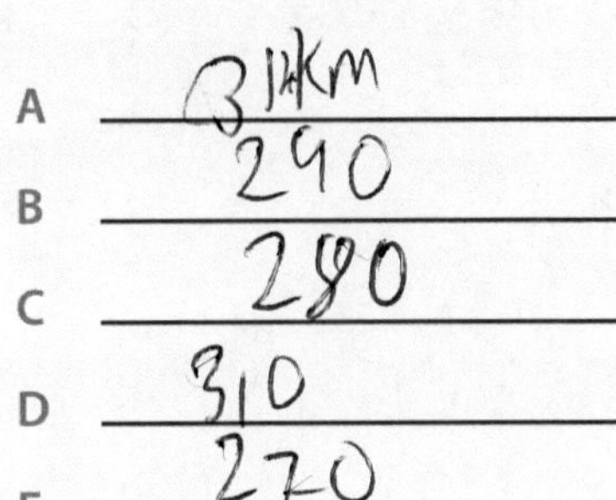

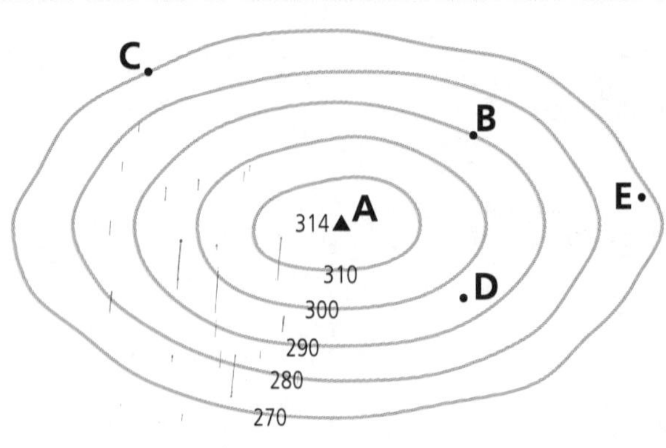

⑱ Refer to the Caher map on page 68 and answer the questions that follow.

(a) What is the height in metres of the peak of Slieveanard? ____________

(b) What is the height of the highest point on the map? ____________

(c) How many mountain tops are more than 500m in height? ____________

(d) How is height shown at S 005 264? ____________

⑲ Refer to the Glencolumbkille map on page 66 and circle the correct answer in each statement.

(a) The highest point on the map is at height of *495m / 595m / 695m*.

(b) Lough Unna is at a height of *126m / 144m / 215m*.

(c) The height above sea level of the Promontory Fort (G 564 843) is *140m / 150m / 160m*.

(d) The zone of forest at G 57 78 lies between the river and the *100m / 150m / 200m* contour.

(e) The highest point of the island in Lough Unshagh (G 549 818) is just above *140m / 150m / 160m*.

Slope and height

⑳ Identify each of the following slope types.

21 Identify each of the following slope types.

A ____________________

B ____________________

C ____________________

22 In the boxes provided, match each letter in column X with the number of its pair in column Y.

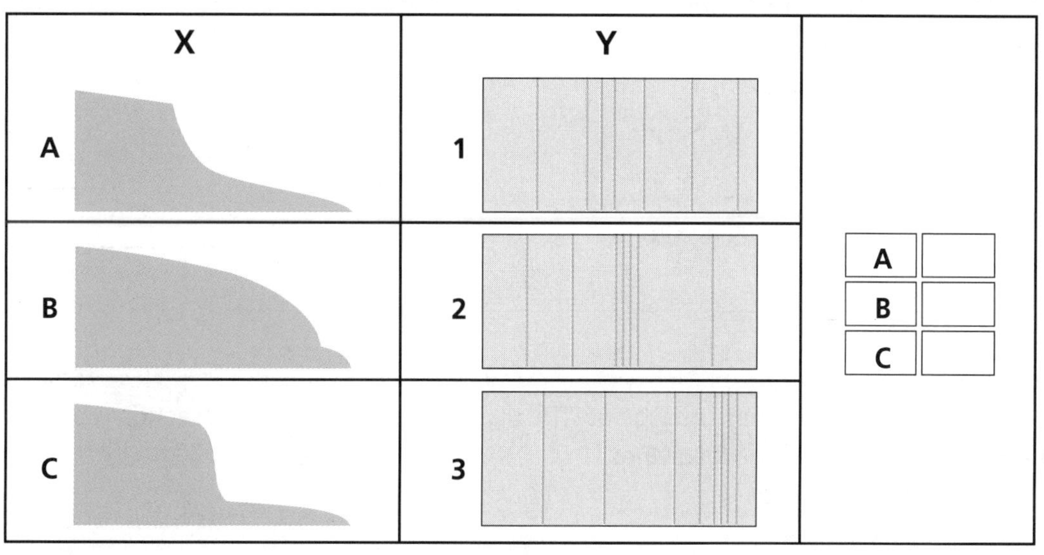

23 Refer to the Caher map extract on page 68 and select the grid square with the steepest slope in each of the following pairs.

(a) R 95 26 S 02 24 ____________________

(b) S 02 22 S 01 23 ____________________

(c) S 01 26 S 01 27 ____________________

24 Refer to the Glencolumbkille map on page 66 and identify the type of slope at each of the following locations.

(a) G 56 77 ____________________

(b) G 58 80 ____________________

(c) G 52 80 ____________________

25 Refer to the Caher map extract on page 68. Identify the spot height .597 (at R 957 256) and spot height .505 (at R 978 255).

(a) Calculate the difference in height between the two points. ____________

(b) Measure the distance between the two points. ____________

(c) Hence, calculate the average gradient between the two points.

26 Refer to the Glencolumbkille map extract on page 66. Calculate the average gradient between .238 (at G 555 836) and .305 (at G 575 836).

Cross sections

27 Refer to the Glencolumbkille map on page 66. The diagram below is of a cross section drawn from G 520 800 to G 600 800. Find the following:

(a) The height at A ____________

(b) The vegetation at B ____________

(c) The name of the river at C ____________

(d) The name of the mountain at D ____________

(e) The road name at E ____________

(f) The road type at F ____________

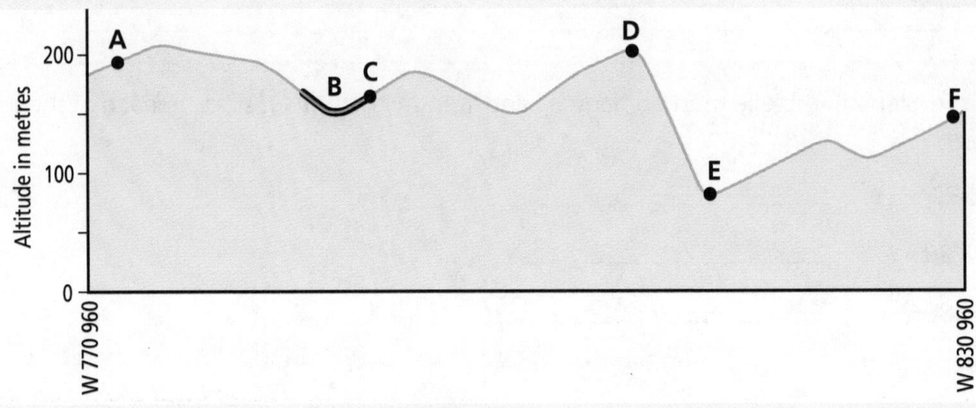

Sketch maps

28 Refer to the Kells map extract on page 64. Show and identify the following features on the sketch map provided.

- R194
- R163
- River Blackwater
- Built-up area of Kells
- Mullagh
- An area of woodland
- A named antiquity

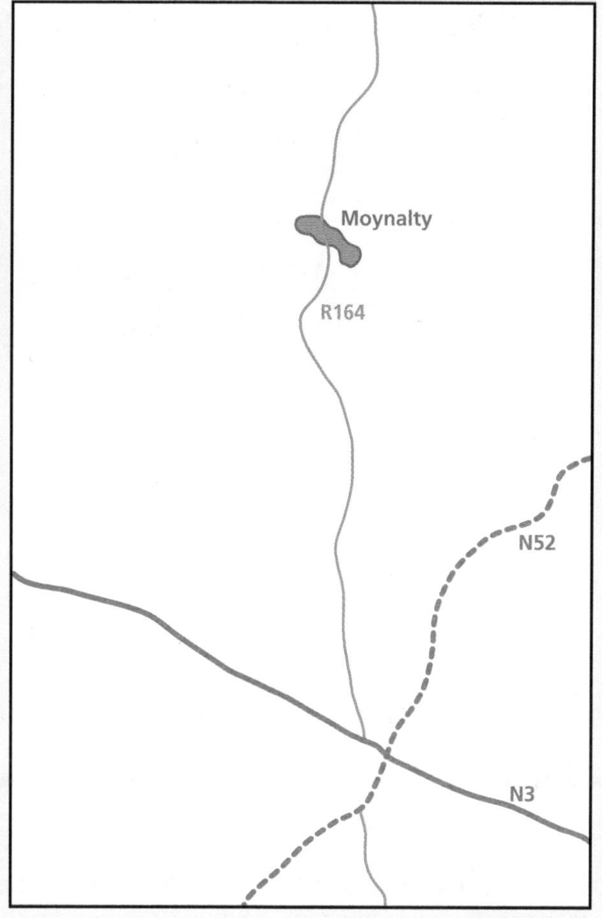

29 Refer to the Timoleague map extract on page 70. Identify and name the features shown on the sketch map.

(a) The road type at A ____________

(b) The river at B ____________

(c) The antiquity at C ____________

(d) The tourist attraction at D

____

(e) The headland at E ____________

(f) The coastal landform at F

____

(g) The type of vegetation at G

____

(h) The accommodation at H

____

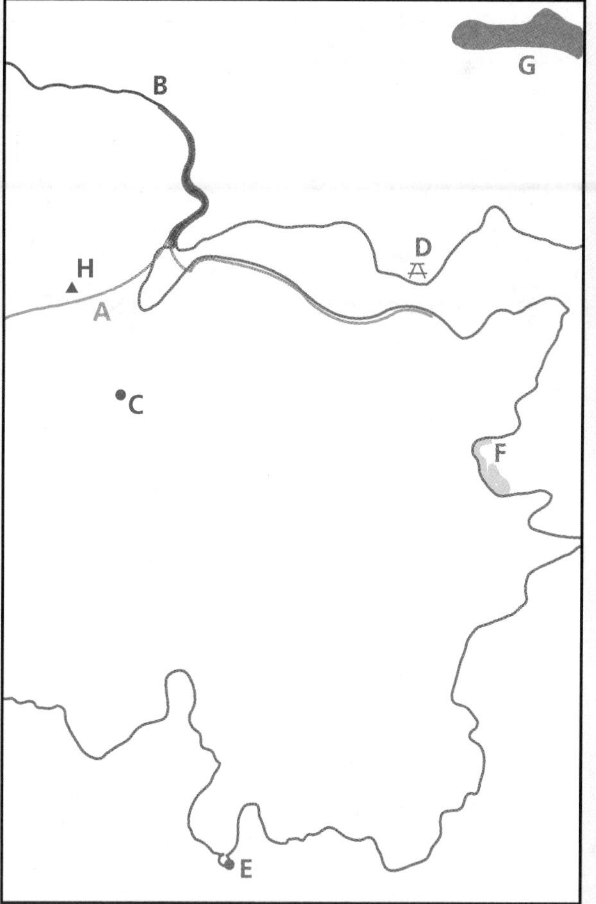

30 Refer to the Caher map extract on page 68. Show and identify the following features in the space provided.

(a) The M8 (b) The built-up area of Caher (c) The River Suir (d) A peak over 500m in height

(e) The Rifle Range (f) The railway (g) A golf course (h) A lake

7.2 Reading the physical landscape

1 Refer to the Caher map on page 68. Link each feature in column 1 with its grid reference in column 2.

Column 1		Column 2	
A	Confluence		R 968 292
B	Meander		R 966 245
C	Floodplain		S 003 297
D	V-shaped valley		S 03 28

2 Refer to the Glencolumbkille map extract on page 66. Link each feature in column 1 with its grid reference in column 2.

Column 1		Column 2	
A	G 567 784		Plateau
B	G 581 805	A	Ridge
C	G 544 784		Hill
D	G 595 785		Gap
E	G 565 835		Mountain
F	G 578 844		Lowland

3 Refer to the Timoleague map on page 70. Link each feature in column 1 with its grid reference in column 2.

	Column 1
A	Sandy beach
B	Cliffs
C	Bay
D	Headland

	Column 2
	W 515 380
	W 516 406
	W 481 354
	W 520 392

Drainage

4 Refer to the Caher map on page 68.

(a) List two pieces of evidence that suggest that the land at S 01 22 is badly drained.

(i) ____

(ii) ____

(b) List two pieces of evidence that suggest that the land at S 06 26 is well-drained.

(i) ____

(ii) ____

7.3 Reading the human landscape

Communications

1 Refer to the Caher map on page 68. Link each grid reference in column 1 with its map feature in column 2.

	Column 1
A	S 021 240
B	S 010 290
C	S 020 283
D	S 045 230
E	S 024 265
F	R 960 287
G	S 054 251
H	S 061 275

	Column 2
	Railway line
	Third class road
	National Primary Road
	Motorway
	Regional road
	Railway Station
	Roundabout
	Waymarked Walk

2. Refer to the Glencolumbkille map on page 66. Describe a journey from Carrick to Glencolumbkille, using these headings:

- Road type: ______________________________
- Direction: ______________________________
- Relief: ______________________________
- Third class roads: ______________________________

3. Refer to the Caher map extract on page 68. Discuss the statement that Caher is served by a well-developed transport network.

____

____

____

____

Settlement

4. Refer to the Timoleague map extract on page 70. Complete the chart below, which refers to ancient settlement in the area shown on the map.

Type of settlement	Example	Grid reference
Defence	Castle	W 491 429
Defence		
Defence		
Burial site		
Burial site		
Worship/religion		
Worship/religion		

5 Examine the diagram below and identify the four patterns of settlement shown.

- Dispersed settlement: ☐
- Absence of settlement: ☐
- Linear settlement: ☐
- Clustered settlement: ☐

6 Refer to the Glencolumbkille map extract on page 66.

(a) Identify the settlement pattern at each of these grid references.

G 55 80 ______________________ G 58 84 ______________________

(b) List two reasons why there is an absence of settlement at G 56 78.

(i) ____

(ii) ____

7 Refer to the Kells map on page 64. Identify and describe any two patterns of settlement in the area shown on the map. Locate each with a grid reference.

(a) Pattern: ______________________ Location: ______________________

Description: ____

(b) Pattern: ______________________ Location: ______________________

Description: ____

8 Refer to the Caher map on page 68. Circle the correct answer in each of the following statements:

(a) Caher is located at a crossing point on a *river / lake* at *S 050 258 / S 050 248*.

(b) The town is built at the point where the river becomes *wider / narrower*.

(c) Caher developed where a number of *regional / national* roads met, such as the *R670 / N24*.

(d) Caher is built on the *50m / 150m* contour.

(e) A railway station is located at the *centre / outskirts* of the town.

9 Refer to the Kells map on page 64. Write three statements to describe the location of Kells.

(a) ______________________________

(b) ______________________________

(c) ______________________________

Urban functions

10 Refer to the Kells map on page 64. Describe the services available in the town, using the following headings:

Service	Example	Location
Education		
Religion		
Accommodation		
Tourism		

11 Refer to the Caher map extract on page 68. Complete the following chart, which refers to some of the functions provided in and around Caher.

Function	Example	Location
Tourist		
		M8, N24, R670
		S 054 251
	Golf Course	
Educational		
		S 055 248
	Youth Hostel	
Religious		

12 Refer to the Caher map extract on page 68. Identify and describe two former functions of Caher.

(a) ______________________________

(b) ______________________________

Land use, tourism and leisure

13 Refer to the Kells map on page 64. Identify the land use at each of the following locations:

N 755 765: ____________ N 760 794: ____________

N 757 758: ____________ N 703 820: ____________

14 Refer to the Timoleague map on page 70. Imagine a tourist visiting the area. Describe its attractions, using the following headings. Support your answer with map evidence.

(a) Accommodation: ____________

(b) Antiquities: ____________

(c) Coast: ____________

(d) Recreation: ____________

15 Refer to the Glencolumbkille map on page 66. Describe any three reasons why the area shown on the map is attractive to tourists. Use map evidence to support your answer.

(a) ____________

(b) ____________

(c) ____________

16 Refer to the Kells map on page 64. Describe any three reasons why the area shown on the map is attractive to tourists. Use map evidence to support your answer.

(a) ____________

(b) ____________

(c) ____________

Placenames

17 Refer to the Glencolumbkille map on page 66. State one piece of information that is suggested by each of these placenames.

(a) Carrick (G 590 790): ____________________

(b) Glencolumbkille (G 530 846): ____________________

(c) Kilgoly (G 550 854): ____________________

7.4 Aerial photographs

1 Examine the aerial photograph of Caher on page 69. Circle the correct location of each of the following features.

(a) Castle: *Right middle / right foreground / centre middle*

(b) Playing field: *Right background / right foreground / left middle*

(c) Town square: *Left middle / centre background / right foreground*

(d) Mill and grain silos: *Right foreground / left background / centre foreground*

2 Examine the aerial photograph of Timoleague on page 71.

(a) Identify the type of photograph and explain your answer.

____

____

____

(b) Identify the location of each of the following features.

- Church: ____________________
- Playground: ____________________
- Abbey ruins: ____________________
- Mudflats: ____________________

3 Examine the vertical aerial photograph and identify the direction of the arrows.

A ____________________

B ____________________

C ____________________

D ____________________

E ____________________

F ____________________

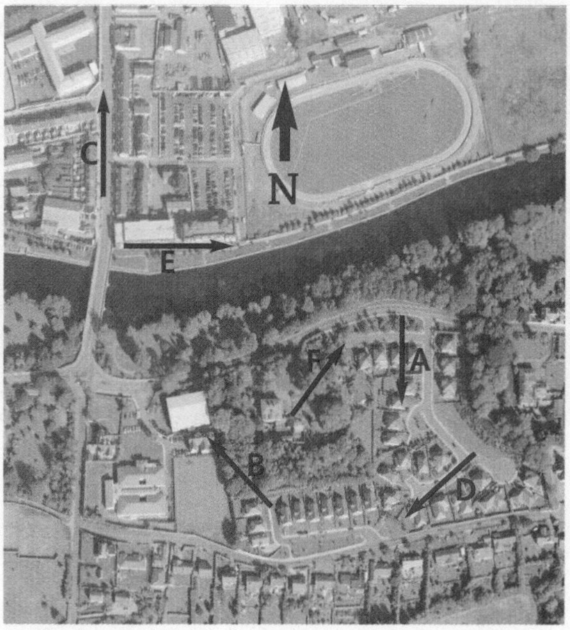

4 Examine the aerial photograph of Caher on page 69.

(a) Identify the season. ____________________

(b) Give two reasons why you selected that answer.

(i) ____________________

(ii) ____________________

5 The sketch map shows some of the features on the aerial photograph of Clonakilty on page 67. Link each feature with its correct letter.

Ornamental garden ☐

Church ☐

Terrace of houses ☐

Clump of trees ☐

Car park ☐

Street with shops ☐

Graveyard ☐

Shed ☐

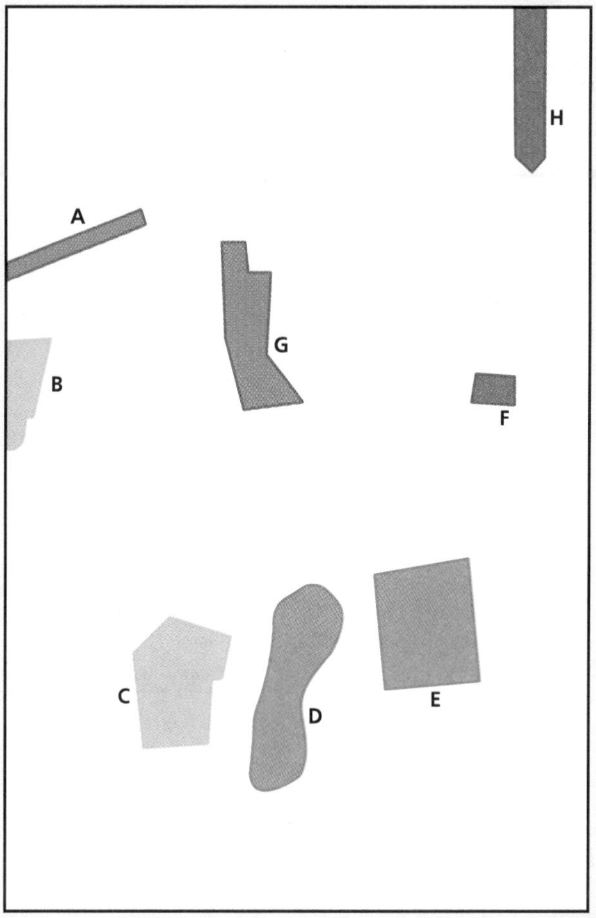

6 Examine the aerial photograph of Kells on page 65. Draw a sketch map. On it show and name the following:

(a) Two roads
(b) The river
(c) The castle
(d) A playing field
(e) A church
(f) A cluster of houses
(g) A car park

7.5 Rural settlement and land use

1 Examine the aerial photograph of Timoleague on page 71. Identify the land uses shown on the sketch map by linking each to its correct letter.

Pastoral farming	☐
Arable Farming	☐
Waste ground	☐
Residential	☐
Transport	☐

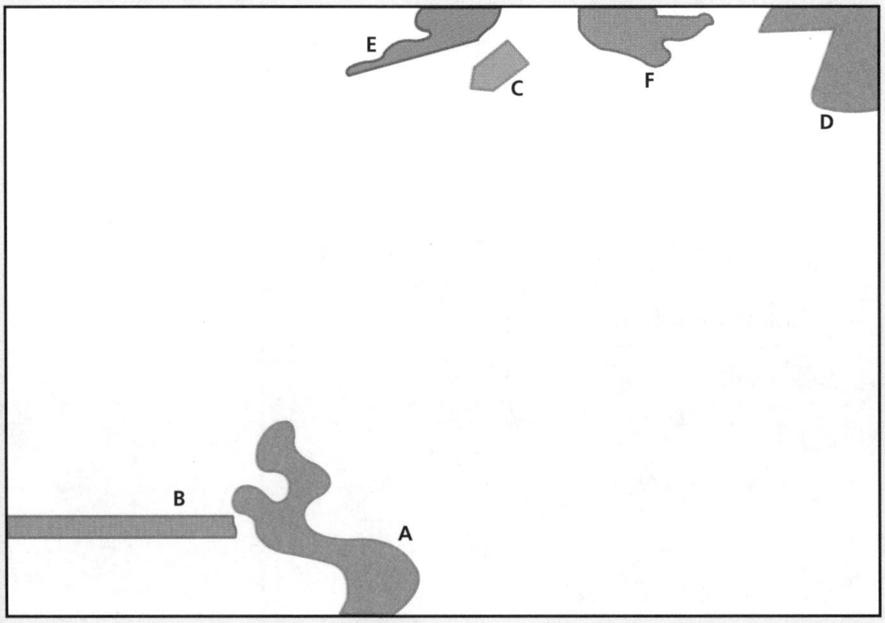

2 Examine the aerial photograph of Caher on page 69. Identify and describe any two rural land uses.

(a) ______________________________

____

____

(b) ______________________________

____

____

7.6 Urban settlement

1 Examine the aerial photograph of Caher on page 69. Describe two reasons why the town developed at this location.

(a) ______________________________

____

____

(b) ______________________________

____

____

2 Examine the aerial photograph of Timoleague on page 71. Describe two reasons why the town developed at this location.

(a) ______________________________

____

____

(b) ______________________________

____

____

3 Examine the aerial photograph of Clonakilty on page 67 and complete the following table.

Function	Evidence in photograph	Location
Residential		
Recreational		
Retail		
Religious		
Transport		
Industrial		

4 Examine the aerial photograph of Timoleague on page 71. Identify and describe three land uses in the photograph.

(a) ______

______

(b) ______

______

(c) ______

______

5 Examine the aerial photograph of Caher on page 69. Identify and locate any three urban functions of the town.

(a) ______

______

(b) ______

______

(c) ______

______

6 Examine the aerial photograph of Caher on page 69.

(a) Identify and locate the main retail street in Caher.

____

(b) What evidence suggests that this is the main shopping area in the town?

(i) ______________________________

(ii) ______________________________

(c) Briefly describe one advantage and one disadvantage of living along the main shopping street of a town such as Caher.

Advantage:

____

____

Disadvantage:

____

____

7 Examine the aerial photograph of Caher on page 69. Identify and describe any two tourist attractions that the town offers for tourists.

(a) ______________________________

____

(b) ______________________________

____

8 Examine the aerial photograph of Clonakilty on page 67.

(a) Identify one location where you think traffic congestion might occur.

____

(b) Give two reasons why you selected this location.

(i) ______________________________

(ii) ______________________________

9. Examine the aerial photograph of Caher on page 69. Identify any two ways that traffic management is used to reduce traffic problems in the town.

(a) ______________________________

____

(b) ______________________________

____

10. Examine the aerial photograph of Caher on page 69. Identify and briefly describe any three house types or residential units shown in the photograph.

(a) ______________________________

____

(b) ______________________________

____

(c) ______________________________

____

11. Examine the aerial photograph of Timoleague on page 71. Imagine that you applied for planning permission to build houses in the land in the left foreground. Describe one advantage and one disadvantage of that site.

Advantage:

____

____

Disadvantage:

____

____

12. Examine the aerial photograph of Caher on page 69. It is proposed to build a hotel in the area shown on the photograph.

(a) Identify a suitable location for the hotel.

____

(b) Describe two reasons why you selected that site.

(i) ______________________________

____

(ii) ______________________________

____

7.7 Comparing maps and photographs

1. Refer to the Caher map extract (page 68) and aerial photograph (page 69). Using evidence from the map and photograph, describe three reasons why the town of Caher developed at this location.

(a) ______________________________

____

(b) ______________________________

____

(c) ______________________________

____

2. Refer to the Kells map extract (page 64) and aerial photograph (page 65). Imagine that you are a tourist visiting the town. Using the map and photograph, describe two attractions for tourists in Kells.

(a) ______________________________

____

(b) ______________________________

____

3. Refer to the Timoleague map extract (page 70) and aerial photograph (page 71). Using evidence from the map and photograph, describe three services that are available in the built-up area of Timoleague.

(a) ______________________________

____

(b) ______________________________

____

(c) ______________________________

____

4. Refer to the Caher map extract (page 68) and aerial photograph (page 69). With reference to the map and photograph, describe two ways in which the river has influenced the development of the town.

(a) ______________________________

(b) ______________________________

Chapter 8

Population: Distribution, Diversity and Change

8.1 Population growth

1. In the boxes provided, match each of the letters in column X with the number of its pair in column Y. One match has been made for you.

X		Y	
A	The population of this continent is growing rapidly.	1	The Black Death
B	The population of the world reached this figure in 2009.	2	Africa
C	The population of this continent is growing very slowly.	3	Europe
D	This caused many deaths in the Middle Ages.	4	6.7 billion

X	Y
A	2
B	4
C	3
D	1

2. Examine the graph and answer the following questions:

(a) What was the approximate population of the world in 1800?

1 billion

(b) In what year approximately did the population of the world reach 1.5 billion?

1900

(c) Give one reason why the population of the world fluctuated before 1700.

They had no medicine for disease.

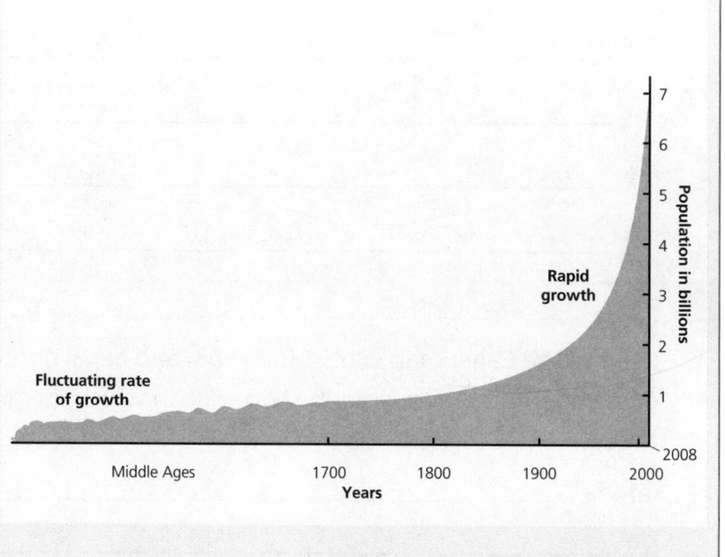

3 Circle the regions from those listed below where population growth is high:

◎ Europe ◎ South Asia ◎ Japan ◎ Africa

4 Examine the diagram and circle the correct answer in each of the following statements:

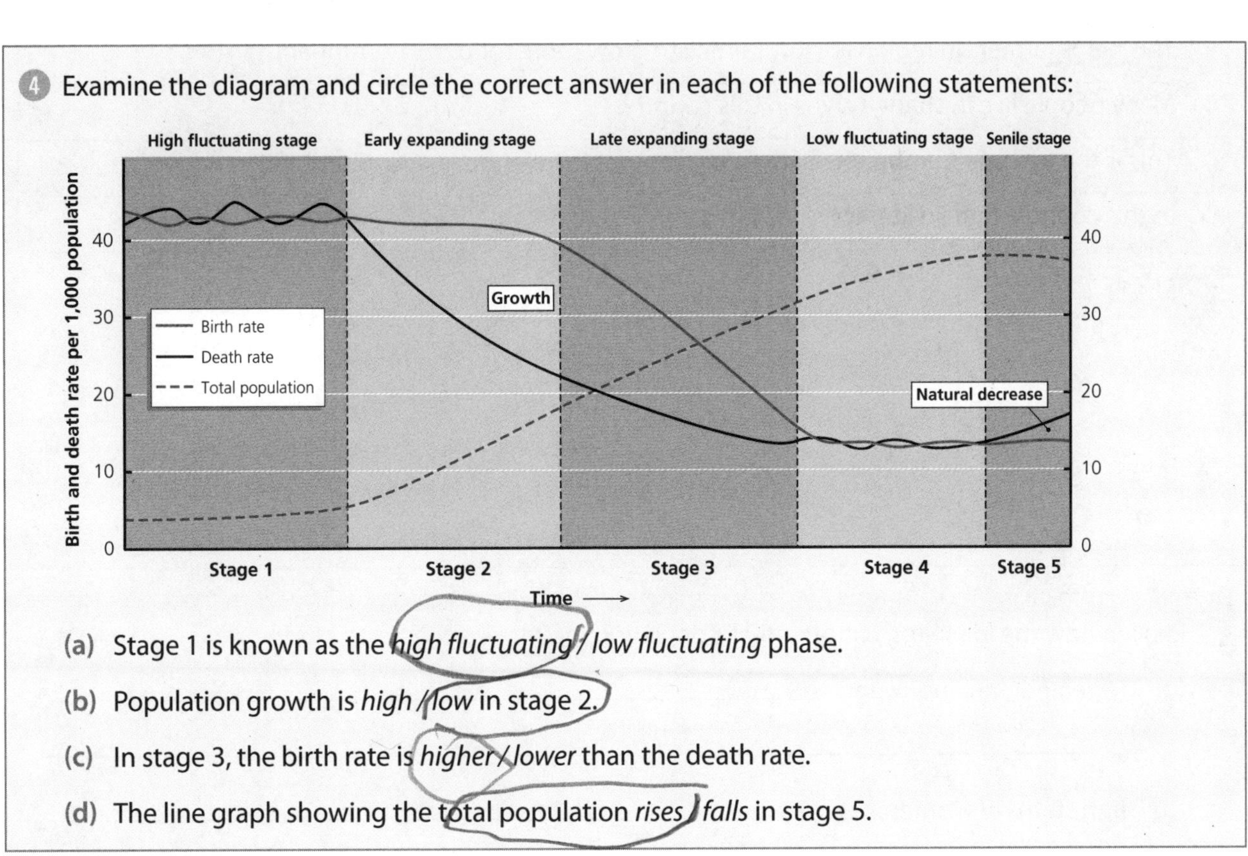

(a) Stage 1 is known as the *high fluctuating* / *low fluctuating* phase.

(b) Population growth is *high* / *low* in stage 2.

(c) In stage 3, the birth rate is *higher* / *lower* than the death rate.

(d) The line graph showing the total population *rises* / *falls* in stage 5.

5 Calculate the annual percentage increase in population in Pakistan using the following information:

(a) Birth rate per thousand in 2006: **50**

(b) Death rate per thousand in 2006: **20**

Annual increase = ____________%

8.2 Factors influencing the rate of population change

1 Read the following statements. Not all the statements are correct.

1 Parents in poor countries tend to have large families.
2 Cholera outbreaks occur frequently in rich countries.
3 Educated mothers tend to plan family size.
4 The population of Brazil grew by 2 million during the years 1900–2007.
5 The population of Ireland increased rapidly before the Great Famine.

Tick the box where all the statements are correct:

2, 4, 5 ☐ 1, 2, 5 ☐ 3, 4, 5 ☐ 1, 3, 5 ☑

2 In the boxes provided, match each of the letters in column X with the number of its pair in column Y. One match has been made for you.

X		Y	
A	This helps farmers in regions of low rainfall to grow more food.	1	Afghanistan
B	Many people live in shantytowns in this country.	2	2.0
C	This is the average number of children per mother in Ireland.	3	Brazil
D	In this country, female literacy is very low.	4	Irrigation

X	Y
A	
B	3
C	
D	

3 Explain how the following factors affect population growth.

(a) Untreated drinking water: ______________________________

____

(b) High status of women: ______________________________

____

(c) War: ______________________________

____

4 Study the bar charts that are shown below and answer the following questions.

(a) What is the female literacy rate in percentages in Brazil?

____

(b) What is the female literacy rate in percentages in Afghanistan?

____

(c) Nepal and Afghanistan are located in which continent?

____

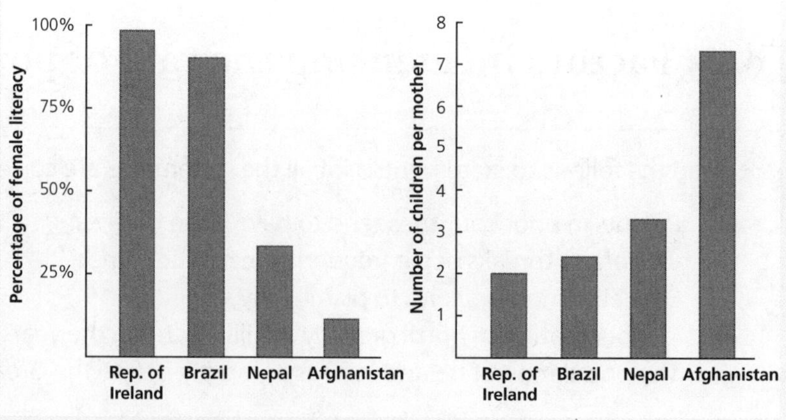

(d) Write down one conclusion that can be drawn from the information in the chart.

____

____

8.3 Future rates of population increase

1 Look at the information below and answer the question that follows.

Population increase per annum	
Year	Additional population
1990	87 million
2002	79 million
2006	77 million

Using the information in the table above, complete the bar chart. One bar has been completed for you.

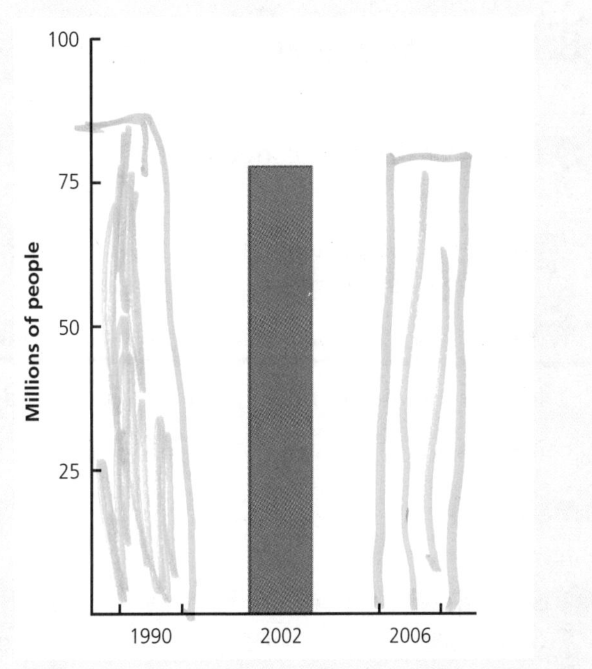

2 In the boxes provided, match each of the letters in column X with the number of its pair in column Y. One match has been made for you.

X		Y	
A	This was the increase in the world's population in 1990.	1	China
B	The world's population increased by this number in 2006.	2	Afghanistan
C	This country is on the threshold of stage 4 of the population cycle.	3	77 million
D	Children provide security for elderly parents in this country.	4	87 million

X	Y
A	4
B	3
C	2
D	1

3 Read the following statements. Not all the statements are correct.

1 Indonesia is very close to stage 4 of the population cycle.
2 Bangladesh has a low birth rate.
3 Parents in poor countries have small families.
4 The world's population grew by 87 million in 1990.
5 Children provide security for ageing parents in poor countries.

Tick the box where all the statements are correct:

1, 2, 3 ☐ 1, 4, 5 ☑ 2, 3, 4 ☐ 3, 4, 5 ☐

8.4 Population pyramids

1 Tick the box with the correct answer.

	True	False
(a) In the Irish population pyramid, there are more elderly males than elderly females.	☑	☐
(b) Irish mothers have an average of two children each at this time.	☑	☐
(c) The German population pyramid has a wide base.	☐	☑
(d) Children aged 4 and under make up almost 10 per cent of the population of Brazil.	☑	☐

2 Study the age / sex pyramids below. One shows the population of a developing country and the other shows the population of a developed country. Answer the questions that follow.

(a) Circle the letter showing the developed country's pyramid: **A** **B**

(b) In country B, what percentage of the population is aged 9 and under? *(Tick the correct box.)*

12% ☐
17% ☑
25% ☐
34% ☐

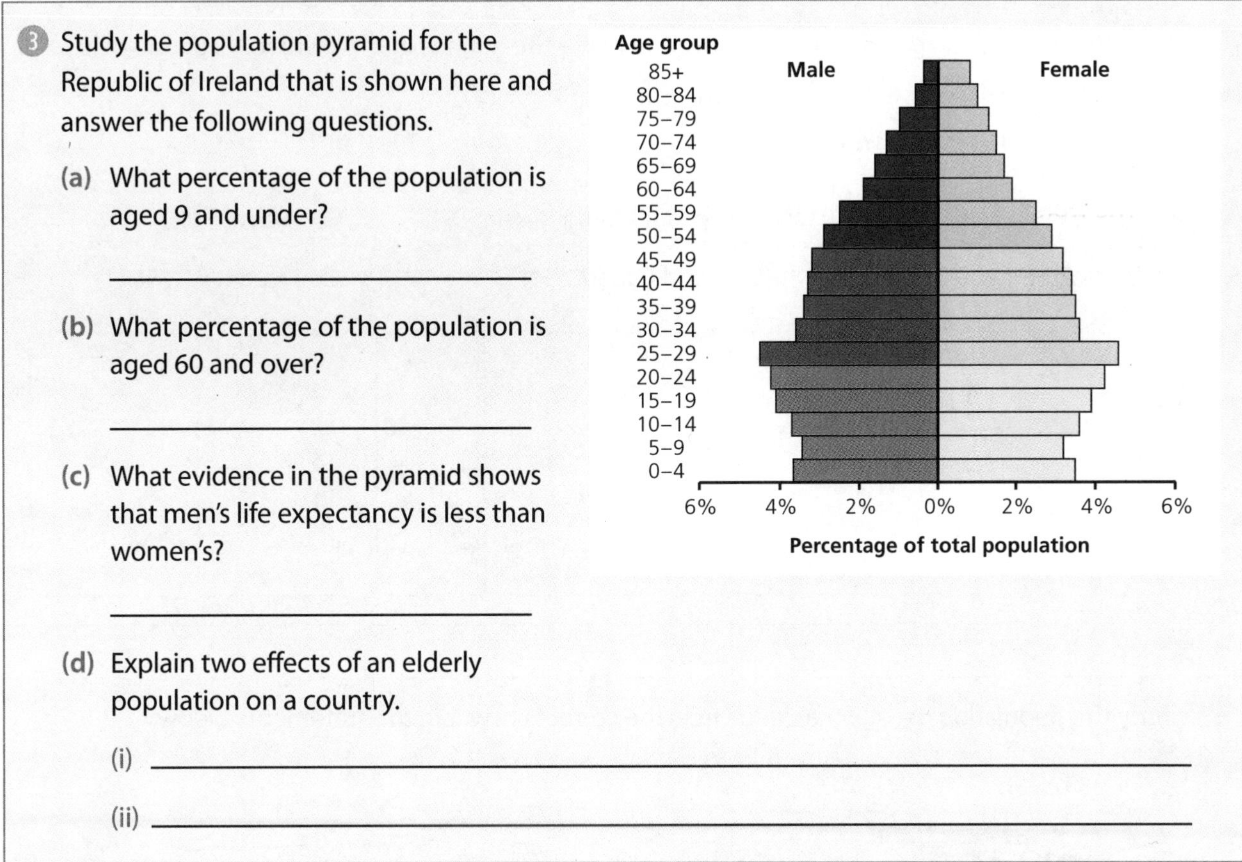

3 Study the population pyramid for the Republic of Ireland that is shown here and answer the following questions.

(a) What percentage of the population is aged 9 and under?

____

(b) What percentage of the population is aged 60 and over?

____

(c) What evidence in the pyramid shows that men's life expectancy is less than women's?

____

(d) Explain two effects of an elderly population on a country.

(i) ____________________

(ii) ____________________

8.5 Variations in population distribution and density

1 In the boxes provided, match each of the letters in column X with the number of its pair in column Y. One match has been made for you.

	X		Y
A	This refers to the average number of people per km².	1	India
B	The Ganges Basin is in this country.	2	Africa
C	Asia has this percentage of the population of the world.	3	Population density
D	This continent has 13% of the world's population.	4	60%

X	Y
A	3
B	1
C	4
D	2

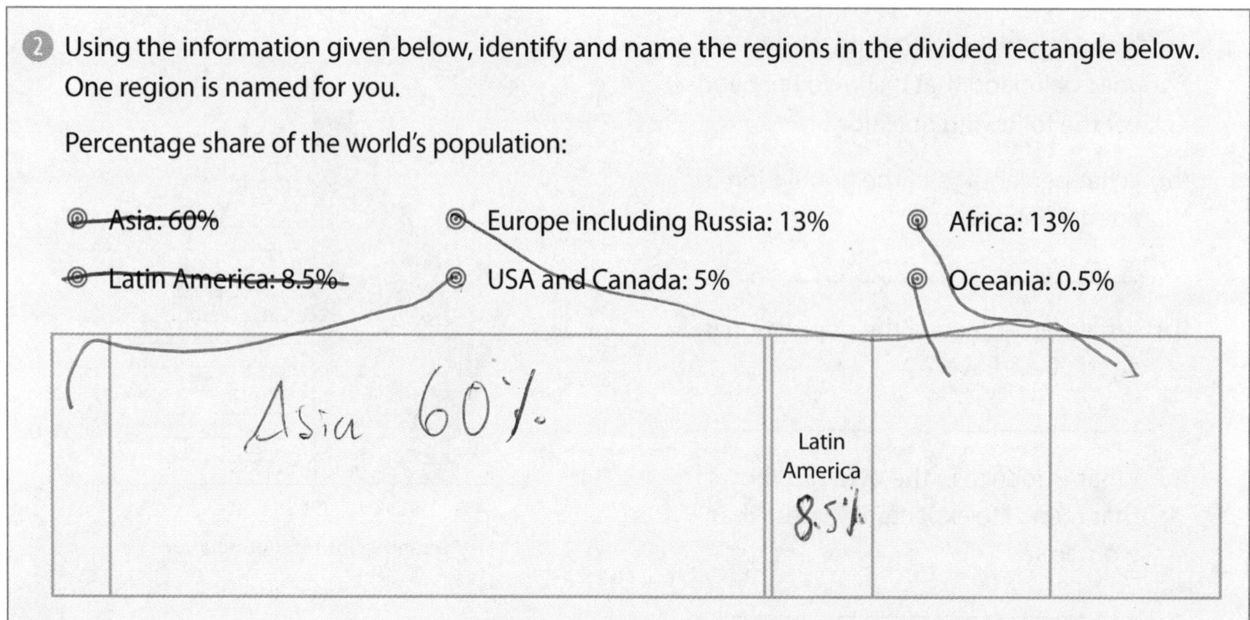

2 Using the information given below, identify and name the regions in the divided rectangle below. One region is named for you.

Percentage share of the world's population:

- ~~Asia: 60%~~
- Europe including Russia: 13%
- Africa: 13%
- ~~Latin America: 8.5%~~
- USA and Canada: 5%
- Oceania: 0.5%

3 Study the population density map and circle the correct answer in the statements below:

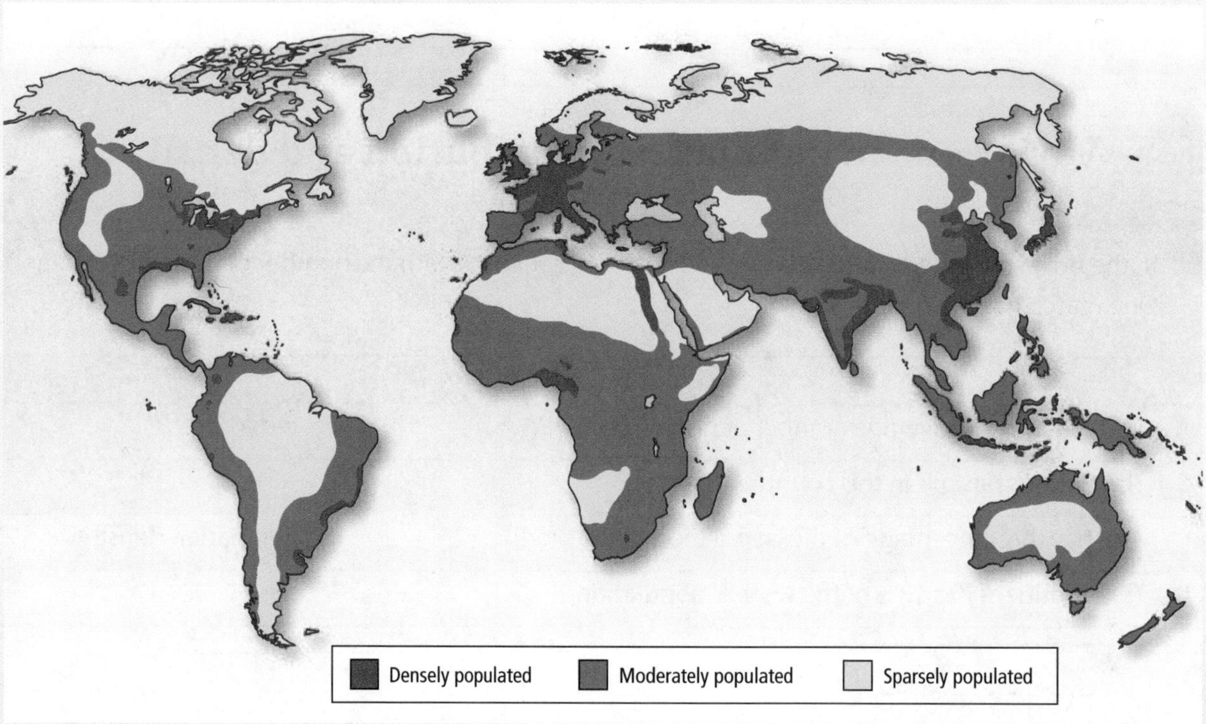

Densely populated
Moderately populated
Sparsely populated

(a) Japan's population density is *high / low.*

(b) Northern Canada's population density is *low / moderate.*

(c) Italy is *densely populated / moderately populated.*

4 Study the information in the bar chart below.

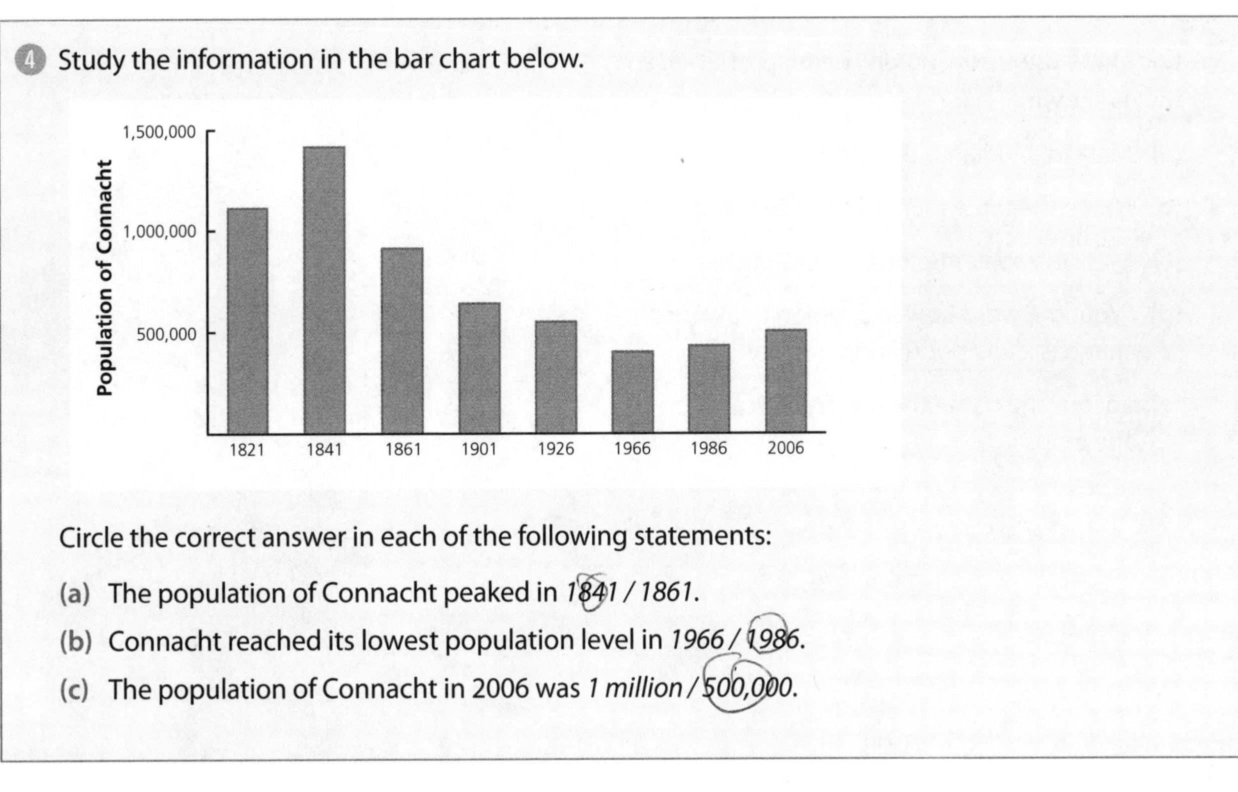

Circle the correct answer in each of the following statements:

(a) The population of Connacht peaked in *1841 / 1861*.

(b) Connacht reached its lowest population level in *1966 / 1986*.

(c) The population of Connacht in 2006 was *1 million / 500,000*.

5 Read the following statements. Not all of the statements are correct.

1 Emigration reduced the population of the West of Ireland for 100 years after the Great Famine.
2 The population of Clifden Rural District has declined steadily since 1911.
3 The population of Galway City was 700,000 in 2006.
4 Scattery Island is still inhabited.
5 The Celtic Tiger years brought jobs to many parts of the West of Ireland.

Tick the box where all the statements are correct:

1, 2, 3 ☐ 3, 4, 5 ☐ 2, 3, 4 ☐ 1, 2, 5 ☑

6 The following passage refers to Brazil. Fill in the blank spaces with appropriate words:

In 2007, the population of Brazil had reached __________ million. The population of Brazil is unevenly __________________. The east coast of Brazil has a very high population ____________. This is partly because the ______________ is suitable for growing coffee and sugar cane. Southern Brazil has cooler ______________ that are very suitable for migrants from ________________ and __________________.

The Amazon Basin has temperatures that are above __________ degrees all __________. However, the interior of Brazil has mineral resources such as __________. The Brazilian ________________ has encouraged people to __________ inland. The interior has become a green ______________ for many settlers. Land becomes infertile because minerals are ____________________ from the soil. Native _____________ have suffered a major reduction in their population because they have poor immunity to European diseases such as _________________________.

7 Complete the following on the map of Sweden that is shown.

(a) Mark in and name the Arctic Circle.

(b) Name the three marked cities in Sweden.

(c) Mark in and name the Gulf of Bothnia.

(d) Write the word **Low** in a region of Sweden that has a low population density.

(e) Locate and name the region of Scania on the map.

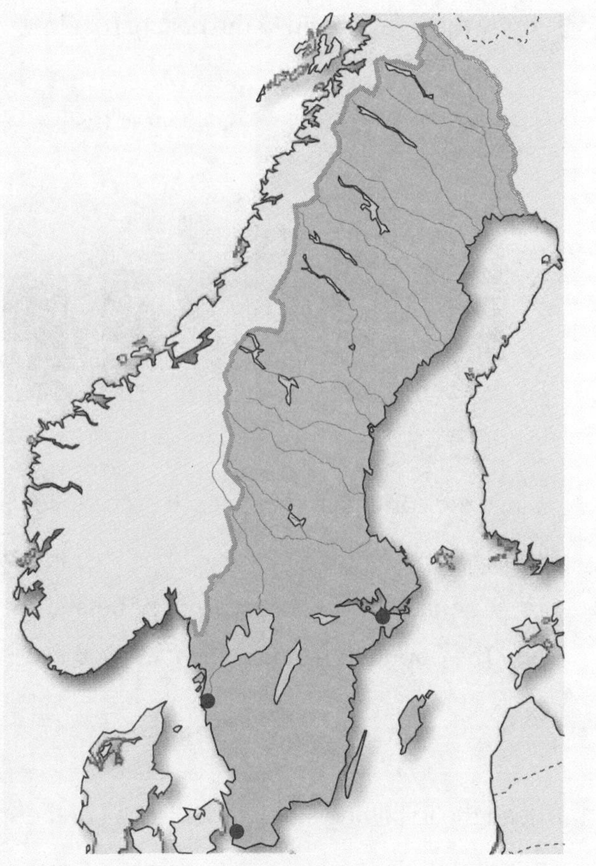

8 Study the temperature graphs for Haparanda (the far north of Sweden) and Malmö (the south of Sweden).

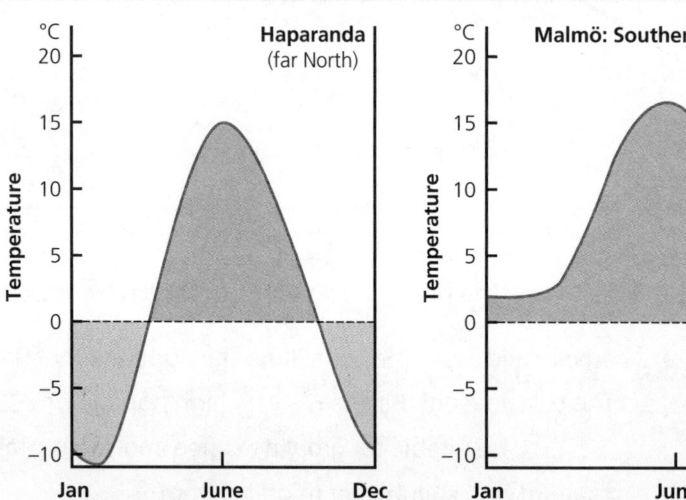

Complete the following table:

	Haparanda	Malmö
January temperature	−10°	2°
June temperature	15°	18°
Number of months above freezing	1	3

8.6 Low population densities

1 In the boxes provided, match each of the letters in column X with the number of its pair in column Y. One match has been made for you.

X	Y
A This person arranged marriages in earlier generations.	1 Dublin
B This has been a major social problem in the West of Ireland.	2 Nineteen
C The people in this city earn above the national average.	3 Emigration
D This is the number of TDs in Connacht.	4 A matchmaker

X	Y
A	
B	
C	
D	2

2 Fill in each of the blank spaces with appropriate words.

The West of Ireland has a ________ population density. ________ migration has caused its population to decline over many decades. In addition, ________ marriage rates in ________ areas of the West reduced the population of many parishes. Some ________ land in the West is now being abandoned. This is because farmers' families are going on to third-level ________. When they qualify, they take up jobs in urban centres such as ________ and ________. The West is also politically ________. The number of TDs in Dublin city and county is more than ________ the number of TDs in all of ________.

3 Complete the following on the map of West Africa.

(a) Shade in and name Mali.

(b) Write the names of three of the neighbouring countries on the map.

(c) Mark in the name of the river that flows through Mali.

(d) Name the city that is marked on the river.

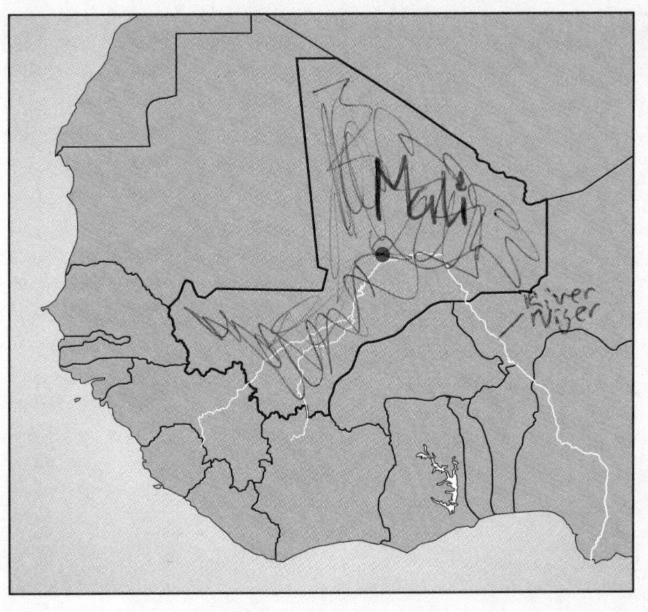

4 Circle the correct answer in each of the following statements:

(a) Mali suffers from frequent *droughts* / *floods*.

(b) The tribes who live in the desert regions of Mali are *nomads* / *settled farmers*.

(c) Mali is a *coastal* / *landlocked* country.

5 Answer the following questions about Mali.

(a) What was the estimated population of Mali in 2007? ____________________

(b) What is the population density of Mali per km^2? ____________________

(c) If the Republic of Ireland is 70,000 km^2, how many times bigger is Mali than the Republic of Ireland? ____________________

(d) Name one environmental problem that exists in Mali. ____________________

6 In the boxes provided, match each of the letters in column X with the number of its pair in column Y. One match has been made for you.

X		Y	
A	A river that flows through Mali.	1	Goats
B	The annual population growth in Mali.	2	Sandstorms
C	These animals are herded by nomads in Mali.	3	The Niger
D	This is a frequent occurrence in Mali.	4	3%

X	Y
A	3
B	4
C	1
D	2

8.7 High population densities

1 Answer the following questions about Kolkata.

(a) Kolkata is located in which country? ______________

(b) Kolkata is located on the banks of which river? ______________

(c) Name two economic activities in Kolkata.

(i) ______________________________

(ii) ______________________________

(d) What was the population of Kolkata in the following years?

1961: ______________

2008: ______________

2 Circle the correct answer in each of the statements below:

(a) Kolkata suffers from *drought / heavy rain* during the monsoon season.

(b) The population of Kolkata has *grown / declined* in recent decades.

(c) Residential districts in Kolkata have *high densities / low densities.*

3 Using the information given, complete the following bar chart. One bar has been drawn for you.

Population growth in Kolkata			
1820	**1931**	**1961**	**2008**
250,000	1.2 m	4.4 m	15.7 m

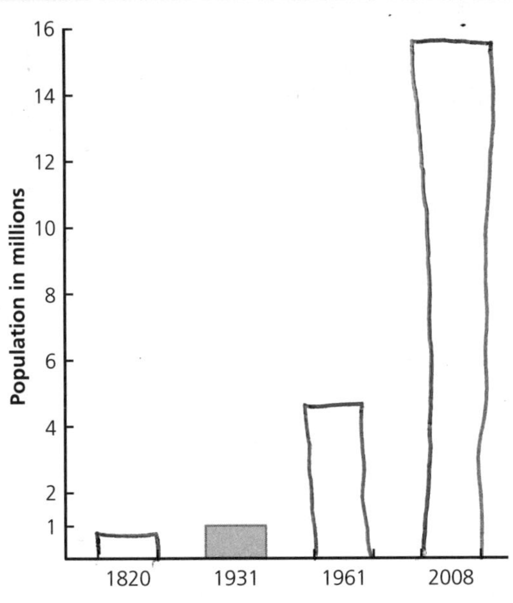

4 Tick the correct box in each case:

	True	False
(a) Hong Kong's population was less than 7 million in 2007.	☑	☐
(b) Most people in Hong Kong live in apartments.	☑	☐
(c) Nobody lives in houseboats in Hong Kong today.	☐	☑
(d) All the beaches around Hong Kong are safe to swim in.	☐	☑
(e) The life expectancy for Hong Kong's population is 82 years.	☑	☐
(f) Hong Kong is a wealthier city than Kolkata.	☐	☑

5 State two ways in which the quality of life is better in Hong Kong than it is in Kolkata.

(a) ______________________________

____

____

(b) ______________________________

____

____

6 Read the following statements. Not all of the statements are correct.

1 Average income per head in Hong Kong was $26,668 in 2007.
2 Victoria is on Hong Kong Island.
3 Most people in Hong Kong live in boats.
4 Hong Kong has a modern water supply.
5 Everyone in Hong Kong is wealthy.

Tick the box where all the statements are correct:

1, 2, 3 ☐ 3, 4, 5 ☐ 1, 3, 5 ☐ 1, 2, 4 ☑

8.8 Global patterns: The North/South divide

1 Examine the map of infant mortality and answer the following questions:

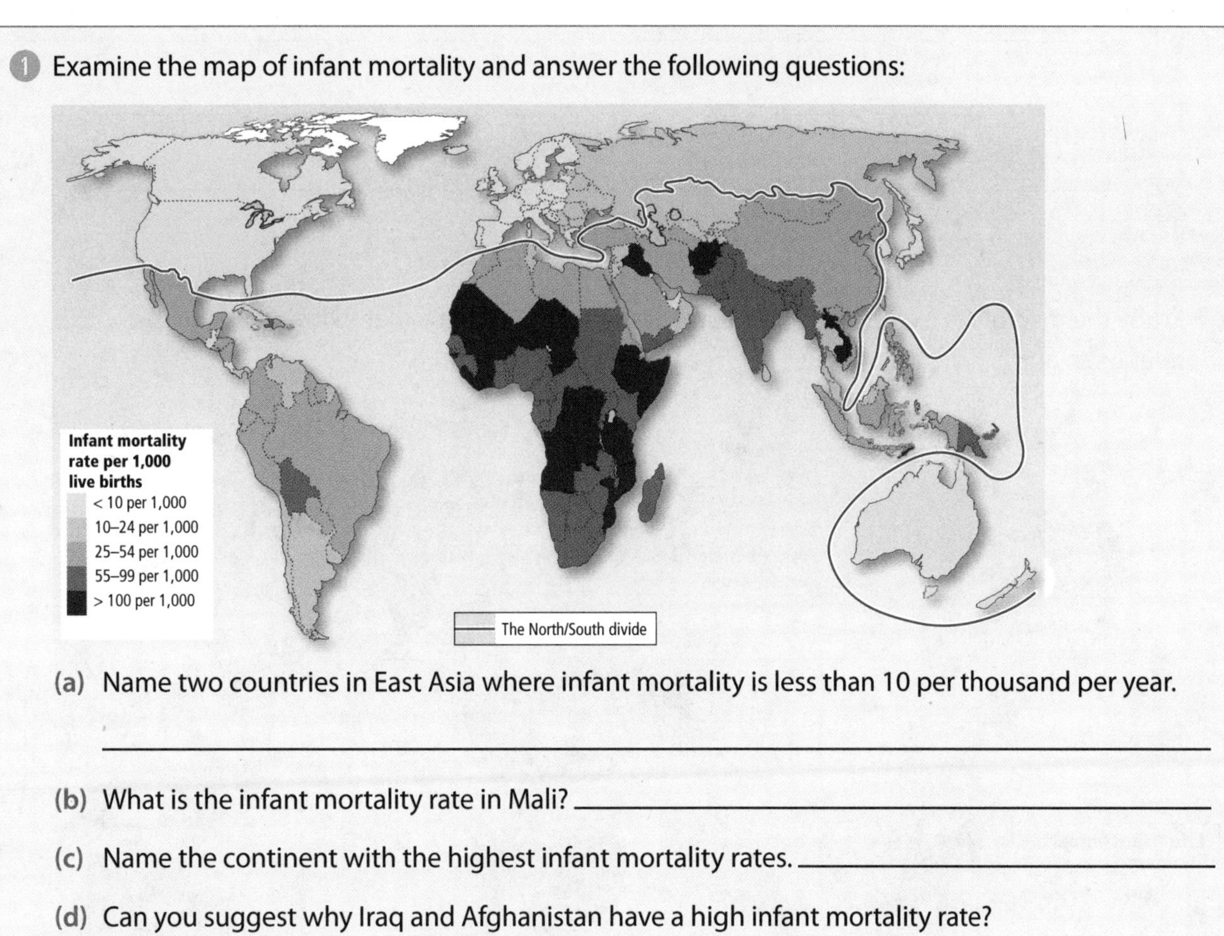

(a) Name two countries in East Asia where infant mortality is less than 10 per thousand per year.

____

(b) What is the infant mortality rate in Mali? ____________________

(c) Name the continent with the highest infant mortality rates. ____________________

(d) Can you suggest why Iraq and Afghanistan have a high infant mortality rate?

____

(e) Name the country with the highest infant mortality rate in South America.

____

2 In the boxes provided, match each of the letters in column X with the number of its pair in column Y. One match has been made for you.

X	Y
A The developed world is also known by this name.	1 Safe drinking water
B This is another name for the South.	2 The North
C This disease causes many children's deaths in the South.	3 The developing world
D An important factor in keeping children healthy.	4 Malaria

X	Y
A	2
B	
C	
D	

3 Explain three reasons why infant mortality is high in many countries of the developing world.

(a) ______________________________

(b) ______________________________

(c) ______________________________

4 Study the map of life expectancy below and answer the questions that follow (you may also need to refer to an atlas):

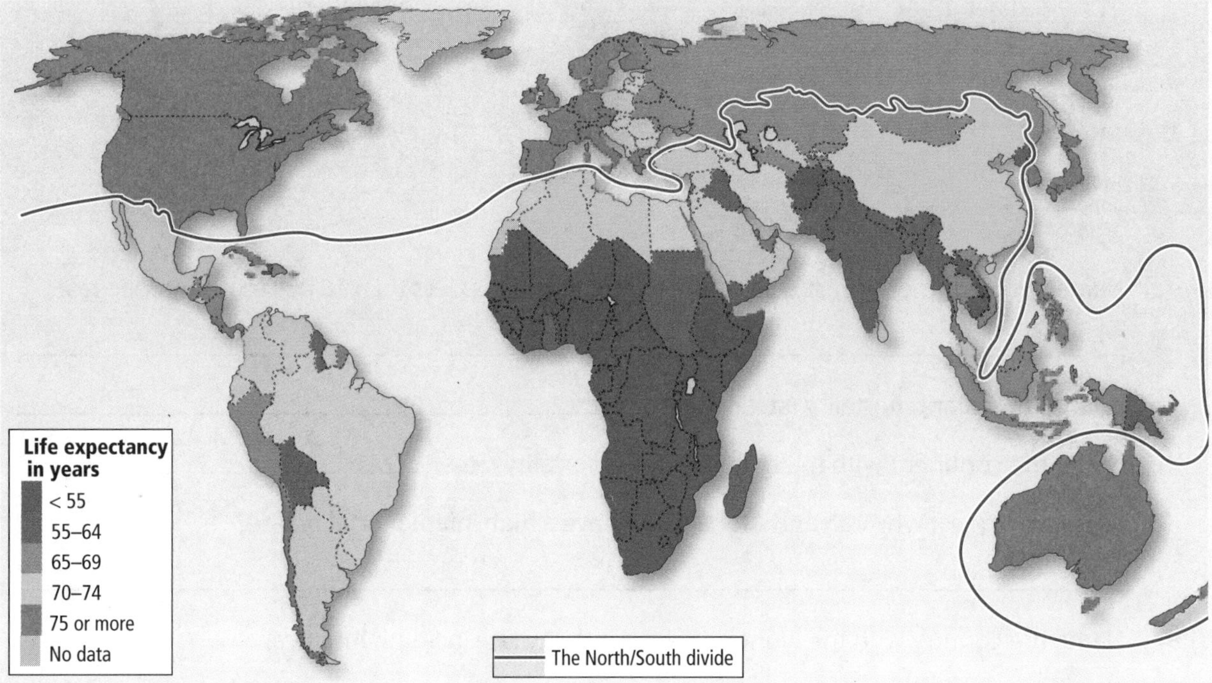

(a) What is the life expectancy in Ireland? ______________________________

(b) Name two countries in East Asia where life expectancy is 75 years or more.

____

____

(c) What region of the world has the lowest life expectancy?

____

(d) Name two countries in Eastern Europe where life expectancy is 70–74 years.

____

____

(e) Why is life expectancy lower in Afghanistan than in surrounding countries?

____

____

5 Circle the correct answer in each of the following statements:

(a) Infant mortality is *very low / high* in the EU.

(b) Life expectancy is *higher / lower* in the USA than in Mexico.

(c) Life expectancy is *rising / falling* in China.

6 Explain three factors that can affect life expectancy in the South:

(a) ______________________________

(b) ______________________________

(c) ______________________________

8.9 People on the move

1 Tick the correct box for each of the statements below:

	True	False
(a) Inward migration began in Ireland after the Great Famine of the 1840s.	☐	☐
(b) People of Irish origin only, migrated into Ireland in recent years.	☐	☐
(c) From 1848 to 1950, 2.5 million people emigrated from Cobh.	☐	☐
(d) More than 400,000 left Ireland in the 1950s.	☐	☐
(e) Economic opportunities in the USA have been a pull factor for Irish emigrants.	☐	☐

2 Read the following passage about Irish immigration patterns from 1950s onward and fill in the blank spaces with appropriate words.

In the 1950s, ______________ emigrated from the Republic of Ireland because of the lack of ______________. However, in the 1960s, during the ______________ emigration was greatly ______________ because the country experienced an economic ______________. Many ______________ were created. In the 1970s, many people who had previously ______________ now returned to ______________.

The economic recession of the 1980s saw outward ______________ resume as people sought their fortunes ______________.

In the mid 1990s, the economic boom known as the ______________ began. Thousands of inward ______________ led to a rapid ______________ in population.

3 Identify two distinct cultural groups that have lived in Ulster since the Plantation of Ulster began.

(a) ______________________________

(b) ______________________________

4 Explain two reasons why the native Irish people of Ulster did not welcome Scottish settlers during the Ulster Plantation.

(a) ______________________________

____

____

(b) ______________________________

____

____

5 (a) Explain why Ulster planters built fortified towns during the Ulster Plantation.

____

____

____

(b) Name two towns built by planters in Ulster.

(i) ______________________________

(ii) ______________________________

6 Explain two results of the Ulster Plantation.

(a) ______________________________

____

(b) ______________________________

____

7 Explain the following terms and give an example of each:

- Organised migration

____

____

____

- Forced migration

____

____

____

- Adventurers

____

____

____

8 Name two European languages that are spoken in South America today.

(a) ______________________________

(b) ______________________________

9 Explain why Portuguese became the language of Brazil.

____

____

____

____

____

Chapter 9

Settlement

9.1 Early settlers in Ireland

1. In the boxes provided, match each of the letters in column X with the number of its pair in column Y. One match has been made for you.

X		Y	
A	Timber paths in early Ireland.	1	Mount Sandel
B	Early settlers crossed into Ireland using these.	2	The Boyne Valley
C	Megalithic tombs are found here.	3	Toghers
D	This early settlement site is in Co. Derry.	4	Land bridges

X	Y
A	☐
B	4
C	☐
D	☐

2. Explain one reason why settlers in Ireland chose crannógs as settlement sites.

____

3. Explain the following terms:

- Middens

____

- Hill forts

____

- Fulachtaí fia

____

- Toghers

____

4 Imagine a tourist asked you about early settlement in your county. Suggest three different examples of historic settlement that you could point to in your reply.

(a) ____________________

(b) ____________________

(c) ____________________

9.2 Nucleated settlements

1 Circle the correct answer in each of the following statements:

(a) Vikings established settlements on the *coast / inland*.

(b) Normans built defensive settlements in the *north-west / south-east* of Ireland.

(c) Virginia, Co. Cavan is a town of *Norman / Plantation origin*.

2 In the boxes provided, match each of the letters in column X with the number of its pair in column Y. One match has been made for you.

X	Y
A Wexford	1 A town of Norman origin
B Fermoy	2 A Plantation town
C Trim	3 A Viking town
D Strabane	4 A town of monastic origin

X	Y
A	☐
B	☐
C	☐
D	2

3 Read the following statements. Not all the statements are correct.

1 The Vikings came to Ireland on land bridges.
2 Clonmacnoise was a monastic settlement.
3 Carrickfergus was founded by the Normans.
4 The Normans introduced castles to Ireland.
5 Cork's population is half of that of Dublin.

Tick the box where all the statements are correct:

1, 2, 3 ☐ 2, 3, 4 ☐ 3, 4, 5 ☐ 1, 2, 4 ☐

4 (a) Explain the term primate city:

(b) Name three primate cities:

(i)

(ii)

(iii

5 Explain the following terms:

- Nucleated settlement
- Plantations
- Commuter belt
- Decentralisation

9.3 Resources, terrain and the distribution of settlement

1 Explain two reasons why people do not settle in high altitudes in Ireland.

(a)

(b)

2 (a) What is the Irish name for each of the following urban centres in Ireland?

- Dublin:
- Athlone:
- Ballina:

(b) What do the Irish names of the towns above have in common?

3 Many nucleated settlements are located along rivers and in river valleys. Give three reasons for this.

(a) ______________________________

____

(b) ______________________________

____

(c) ______________________________

____

4 In the boxes provided, match each of the letters in column X with the number of its pair in column Y. One match has been made for you.

	X		Y
A	This town is located in the fertile lowlands of Co. Kildare.	1	Ballybunion
B	This town is a fishing port in Co. Donegal.	2	Shannonbridge
C	This town in the Midlands has grown as a resource-based settlement.	3	Maynooth
D	This town is a coastal resort in Co. Kerry.	4	Killybegs

X	Y
A	3
B	
C	
D	

5 Examine the photograph of Shannonbridge. Using evidence in the photograph, explain why Shannonbridge is a resource-based settlement.

____

____

____

____

____

____

9.4 Settlements in the new polders of the Netherlands

1 Mark the following places on the map:

- The Barrier Dam
- Emmeloord
- Lake Ijssel
- North-east Polder
- Eastern Flevoland
- A planned polder

Coastline, 1920
Dyke
Dyke under construction
Fresh water
Pumping stations

2 In the boxes provided, match each of the letters in column X with the number of its pair in column Y. One match has been made for you.

X	Y
A This fraction of the Netherlands is below high-tide level.	1 Emmeloord
B This is the name given to land reclaimed from the sea.	2 The Randstad
C This is the market centre of the North-east Polder.	3 One third
D This is an overcrowded part of the Netherlands.	4 A polder

X	Y
A	
B	4
C	
D	

9.5 Functions of nucleated settlement

1 In the boxes provided, match each of the letters in column X with the number of its pair in column Y. One match has been made for you.

X		Y	
A	A dormitory settlement	1	Knock
B	A recreational settlement	2	Navan
C	A resource-based settlement	3	Killarney
D	An ecclesiastical settlement	4	Sixmilebridge

X	Y
A	
B	
C	2
D	

2 Explain the following terms:

- Recreational settlement

____

- Market settlement

____

- Dormitory settlement

____

3 (a) Study the sketch map of the Shannon Basin. Write in the names of the following urban centres that are marked on the map: Carrick-on-Shannon, Athlone, Shannonbridge, Killaloe, Limerick, Foynes.

(b) In the spaces below, write in the names of three important lakes on the River Shannon:

(i) ________________

(ii) ________________

(iii) ________________

(c) Write in one present day function of the following towns:

Athlone ________________

Foynes ________________

Shannonbridge ________________

Killaloe ________________

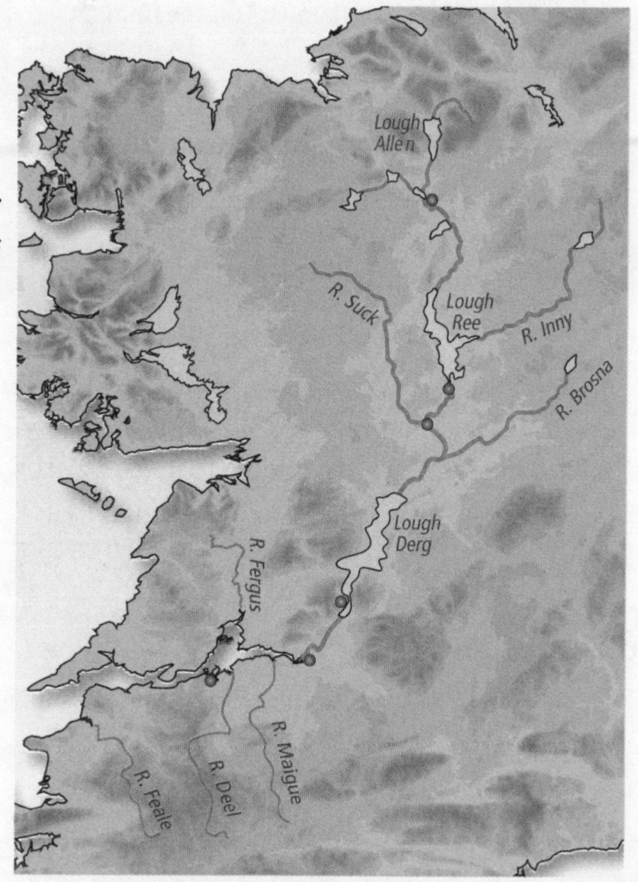

4 Read the following passage and fill in the blanks with appropriate words:

Limerick began as a ________________ settlement. A medieval fortress known as ______________ stands overlooking the Shannon. Because Limerick is located at the lowest __________ __________ of the Shannon, the city has become a route __________. As a result, the city has a ____________ function today. The city also has a residential __________. The population of Limerick has continued to expand because it is close to _________________ Airport and _________________ industrial ________________________. Therefore, in recent decades, many new ____________________ areas have been built on the _____________ of the city.

5 (a) Study the sketch of the River Rhine. Mark in and name the following urban centres:

- Rotterdam
- Köln
- Koblenz
- Rudesheim
- Mainz
- Mannheim
- Ludwigshafen
- Basel

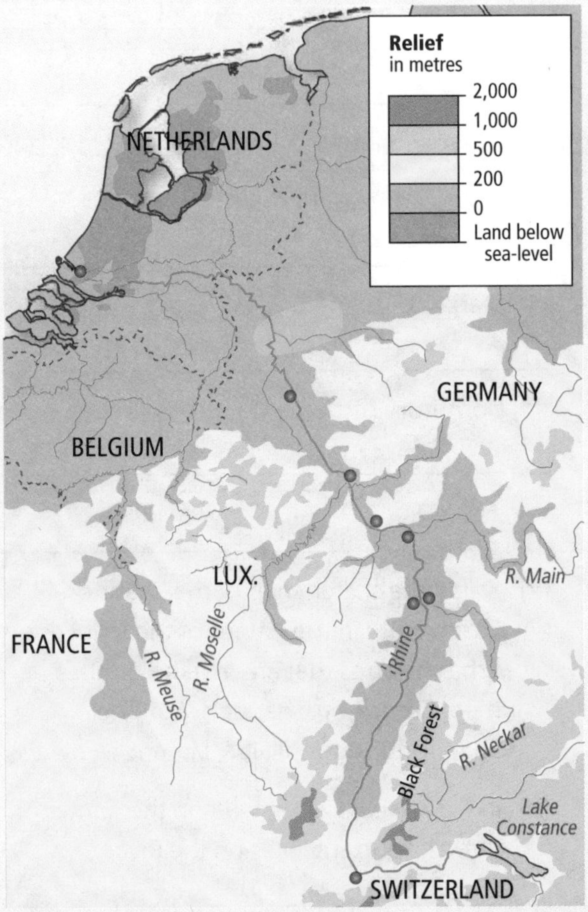

(b) State one important function of each of the following settlements on the Rhine:

Rotterdam: ____________________________

Rudesheim: ____________________________

Köln: ____________________________

6 Read the following passage and fill in the blanks with appropriate words:

Köln is a major urban centre on the river _______________. The city is a major _______________ port. Köln is also a very busy ________________ and ________________ junction. The city has a very important market _______________ today. Many _______________ visit the city. The ________________________ is the most impressive building in Köln. Köln's city centre dates from ____________________ times.

9.6 Change in the function of settlements

1 Read the following statements. Not all of the statements are correct.

1 Navan is located on the River Boyne.
2 An iron mine is located beside Navan.
3 The population of Navan is more than 50,000.
4 Navan now has a dormitory function.
5 Navan no longer manufactures carpets.

Tick the box where all the statements are correct:

1, 2, 3 ☐ 2, 3, 4 ☐ 1, 3, 5 ☐ 1, 4, 5 ☐

2 Explain how Navan acquired two new functions in recent decades.

(a) ______________________________

____

(b) ______________________________

____

9.7 Large-scale industrial development

1 In the boxes provided, match each of the letters in column X with the number of its pair in column Y. One match has been made for you.

X	Y
A This was a former function of Clarecastle.	1 Norman castle
B Clarecastle is at a bridgepoint on this river.	2 Roche
C The manufacturing plant in Clarecastle is owned by this company.	3 Port
D These ruins are located beside Clarecastle.	4 Fergus

X	Y
A	3
B	☐
C	☐
D	☐

2 (a) Explain two functions that Clarecastle had in the past.

(i) ______________________

(ii) ______________________

(b) How did Clarecastle acquire a large-scale industrial function?

____

____

9.8 Communication links

1 The following airports are located beside which European cities?

- Charles de Gaulle: ______________
- Schiphol: ______________
- Gatwick: ______________

2 Tick the correct box in each case:

	True	False
(a) Charles de Gaulle Airport is in Italy.	☐	☐
(b) Heathrow Airport carries 68 million passengers per year.	☐	☐
(c) Dublin Airport is Europe's busiest airport.	☐	☐
(d) The London region has five important airports.	☐	☐
(e) Schiphol Airport is close to Amsterdam.	☐	☐

3 Look at the map of London and its surrounding region.

(a) On the map name five airports in the London region.

(b) Why has London Stansted grown rapidly in recent years?

____

____

____

____

____

____

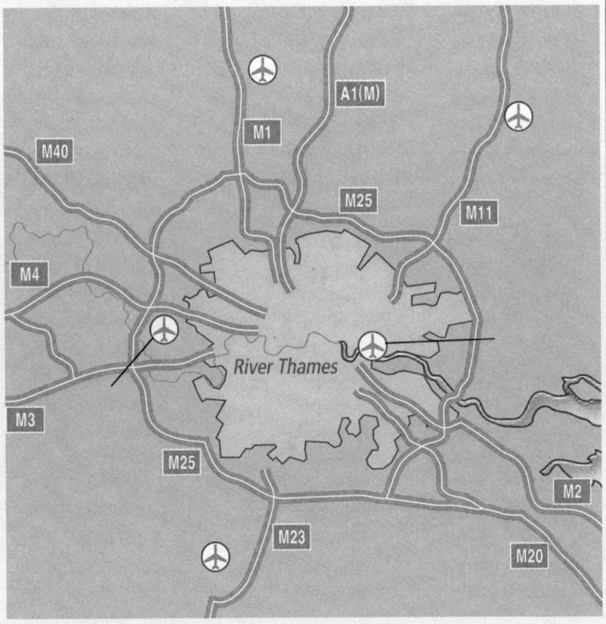

3 (c) Explain two ways in which the economy of London and the London region have benefited from airport activity.

(i) ______________________________

____

____

(ii) ______________________________

____

____

4 On the map of Clare mark in and name the following features:

- Shannon Airport
- Ennis
- Limerick City
- The Shannon Estuary

5 Explain two ways in which the presence of the airport in Shannon is an economic benefit for the surrounding region.

(a) ______________________________

____

(b) ______________________________

____

6 Read the following passage about transport on the River Rhine and fill in the blanks with appropriate words:

The Rhine is Europe's most important navigable __________. One of the world's largest ports __________ is located at its __________ .This port imports __________ materials such as __________ and __________. Every day, __________ travel up and down the river, carrying __________ cargo that includes __________ and __________.

Many heavy __________ are located in the cities that line the __________ of the Rhine.

Chapter 10

Urbanisation

10.1 Changing patterns in where we live: Cities

1. Look at the map of Dublin and complete the following activities:

(a) Mark with a V the location of Viking Dublin.
(b) Write the dates 1900–1970 in part of the area that was built up during those years.
(c) Mark with a P the location of Phoenix Park.
(d) Name Tallaght on the map.
(e) Shade in and name the Dublin Mountains.

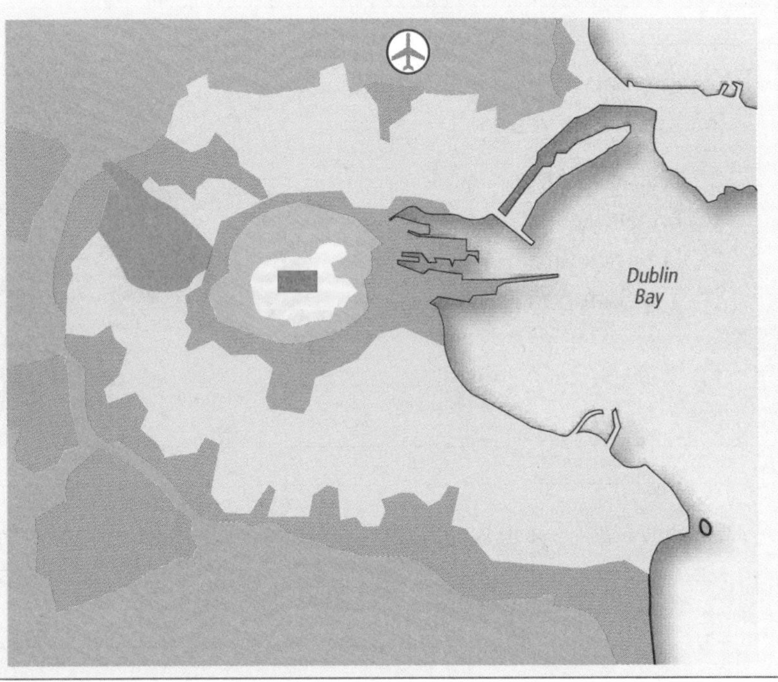

2. In the boxes provided, match each of the letters in column X with the number of its pair in column Y. One match has been made for you.

X	Y
A This building was constructed during the Anglo-Norman era.	1 Merrion Square
B This building was constructed during the reign of Elizabeth I.	2 The Vikings
C This group of invaders built a settlement close to the mouth of the River Liffey.	3 Trinity College
D This square is surrounded by Georgian buildings.	4 Christchurch Cathedral

X	Y
A	
B	
C	
D	1

3 Circle the correct answer in each of the following statements:

(a) A century ago, Dublin tenements were occupied by *wealthy people / poor people*.

(b) Tallaght is located *west / north* of Dublin.

(c) The *Vikings / Normans* were defeated at the Battle of Clontarf.

(d) St Patrick's Cathedral is a *stone / timber* building.

10.2 Cities: Functional zones

1 Study the map of a city. Match the letter with its functional zone in the boxes below. One has been filled for you.

- The CBD [A]
- An out-of-town shopping centre ☐
- An industrial estate ☐
- An industrial area beside the port ☐
- A satellite town ☐
- Open space for recreation ☐

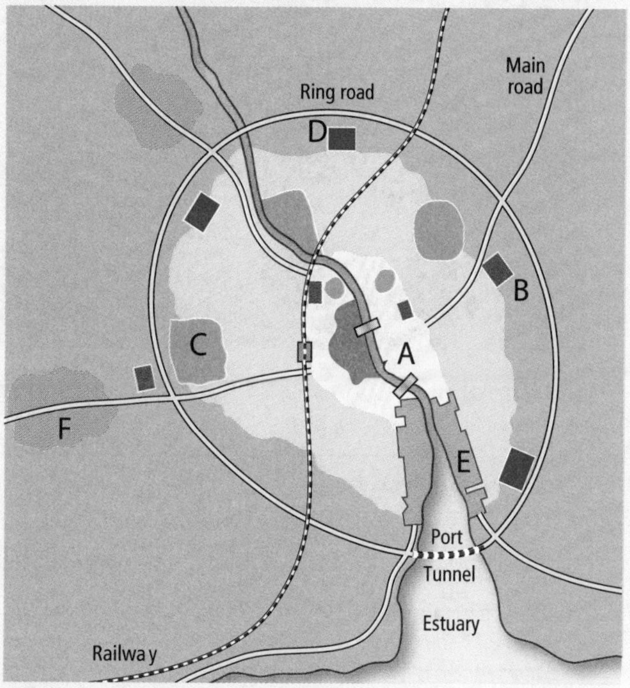

Ring road
Main road
D
B
C
A
F
E
Port
Tunnel
Estuary
Railway

2 In cities, what is the main area or zone for business and shopping called? *(Tick the correct box.)*

(a) The inner city ☐

(b) The shopping centre ☐

(c) The central business district ☐

(d) The business park ☐

3 Which of the following are found in the CBD? *(You may tick more than one box.)*

(a) Office blocks ☐

(b) Community centres ☐

(c) Sports grounds ☐

(d) Department stores ☐

(e) Residential districts ☐

4 Look at the photograph of the Dooradoyle Shopping Centre in Limerick below, and answer the following questions.

(a) The photograph shows different urban land use zones. Write down two of them:

(i) ______________________________

(ii) ______________________________

(b) Do you think that this shopping centre is located close to the centre or on the outskirts of Limerick city? Explain your answer.

____

____

5 In the boxes provided, match each of the letters in column X with the number of its pair in column Y. One match has been made for you.

X		Y	
A	This is the name of the Paris Stock Exchange.	1	Marne-la-Valée
B	This is the name of a university in Paris.	2	The fashion Industry
C	This is where Disneyland Resort, Paris is located.	3	The Paris Bourse
D	This is an important industry in Paris.	4	The Sorbonne

X	Y
A	3
B	
C	
D	

6 Circle the correct answer in each of the following statements:

(a) La Défense is associated with *offices / factories*.

(b) The Champs Elysées is in the *CBD / outskirts of Paris*.

(c) The Champs de Mars is a *city park / residential street*.

(d) The Bois de Boulogne is a *park / residential district*.

7 Why can Paris be called:

(a) A primate city?

____

(b) A world city?

____

10.3 Land values in cities

1 Look at the diagram below and answer the questions.

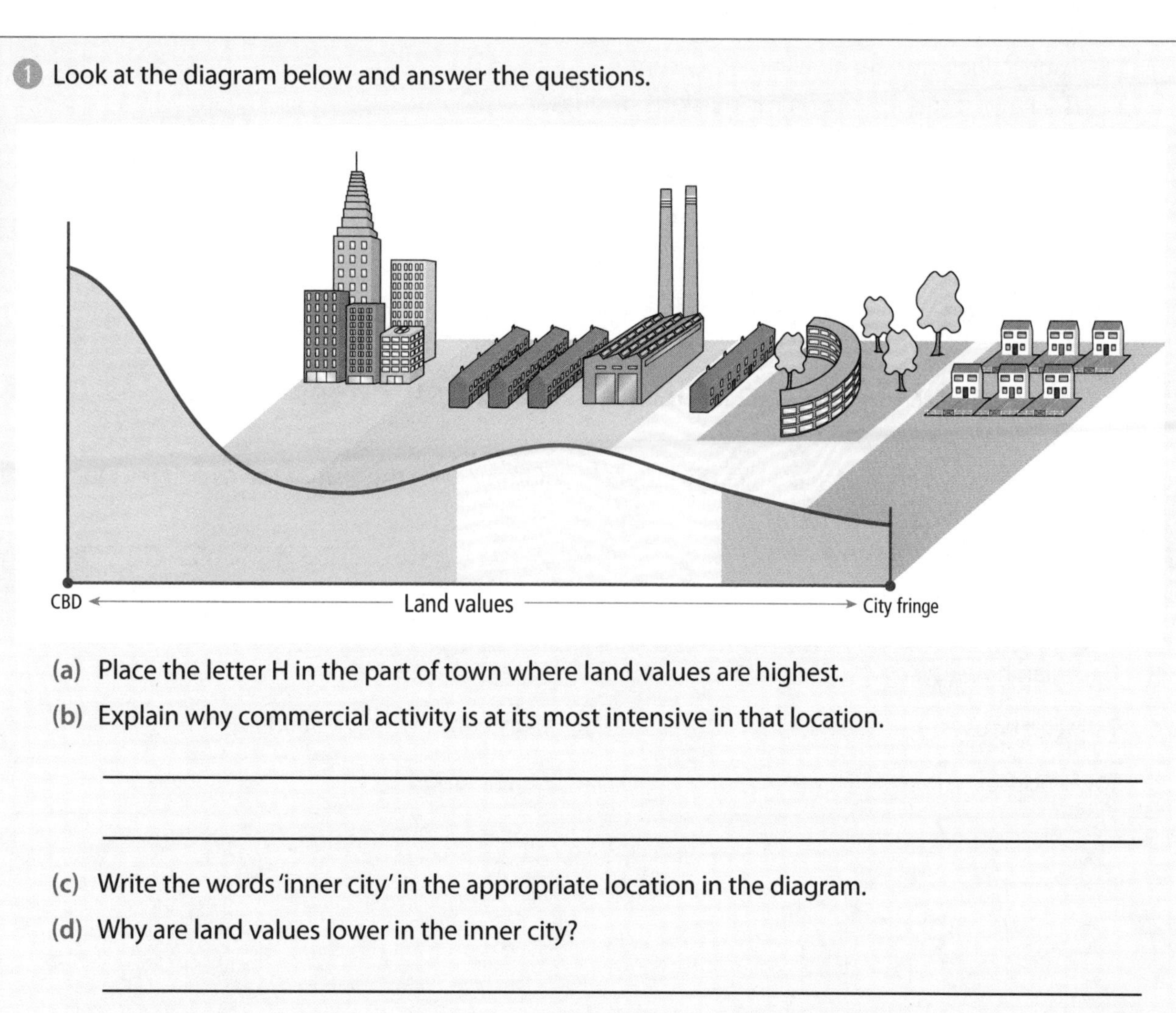

(a) Place the letter H in the part of town where land values are highest.

(b) Explain why commercial activity is at its most intensive in that location.

____

____

(c) Write the words 'inner city' in the appropriate location in the diagram.

(d) Why are land values lower in the inner city?

____

____

2 Which of the following would you **not** find in the CBDs of cities in Ireland? *(Tick the correct box.)*

(a) Travel agencies ☐

(b) Fast food premises ☐

(c) CD stores ☐

(d) Mobile phone outlets ☐

(e) Industrial estates ☐

3 Suppose that you plan to open a computer store that is aimed at the teenage market. Choose the part of a city or town where you would locate your store. State two reasons for your choice.

Location: ______________________

(a) ______________________

(b) ______________________

4 Read the following statements. Not all of the statements are correct.

1 Land values are very high in the city centre.
2 The newest suburbs are on the outskirts of cities.
3 Building height increases away from the city centre.
4 The inner city contains derelict buildings.
5 Land values are higher in the inner city than in the CBD.

Tick the box where all the statements are correct:

3, 4, 5 ☐ 2, 3, 4 ☐ 1, 4, 5 ☐ 1, 2, 4 ☐

10.4 Residential accommodation in Irish cities

1 In the boxes provided, match each of the letters in column X with the number of its pair in column Y. One match has been made for you.

X	Y
A Semi-detached homes	1 Modern houses near the town centre
B Georgian houses	2 Inner suburbs
C Terraced houses	3 Eighteenth-century buildings
D Town houses	4 Outer suburbs

X	Y
A	4
B	☐
C	☐
D	☐

2 Read the following passage and fill in the blanks with appropriate words:

Irish towns and cities have ________ outwards from the centre over ________ of years. Therefore, the oldest ________ are found close to the city centre. For instance, ________ houses with a particular architectural ________ are at least ________ hundred years old. Today, some wealthy people live close to the city centre in ________ houses and in apartment ________. These people work in the nearby ________. Many families live in the suburbs in ________ homes.

3 State one advantage and one disadvantage of living in the outer suburbs of a city in Ireland today.

Advantage: ________

Disdvantage: ________

4 Look at the photograph that shows a city centre apartment block in Limerick. Suggest two reasons why many people have moved into such apartments in recent years.

(a) ________

____

____

(b) ________

____

____

____

5 List three types of accommodation used by people who live in or near city centres:

(a) ________ (b) ________ (c) ________

6 (a) Explain why insulation of homes is very important today.

____

____

(b) List three methods used today to provide insulation in homes.

(i) ________

(ii) ________

(iii) ________

10.5 Commuting to work in cities

1. Explain the following terms:

◎ Commuting journey

___

◎ Rush hour

___

◎ Congestion charges

___

◎ QBCs

___

◎ The DART

___

2. Study the bar chart below. Read the following statements and tick the appropriate box:

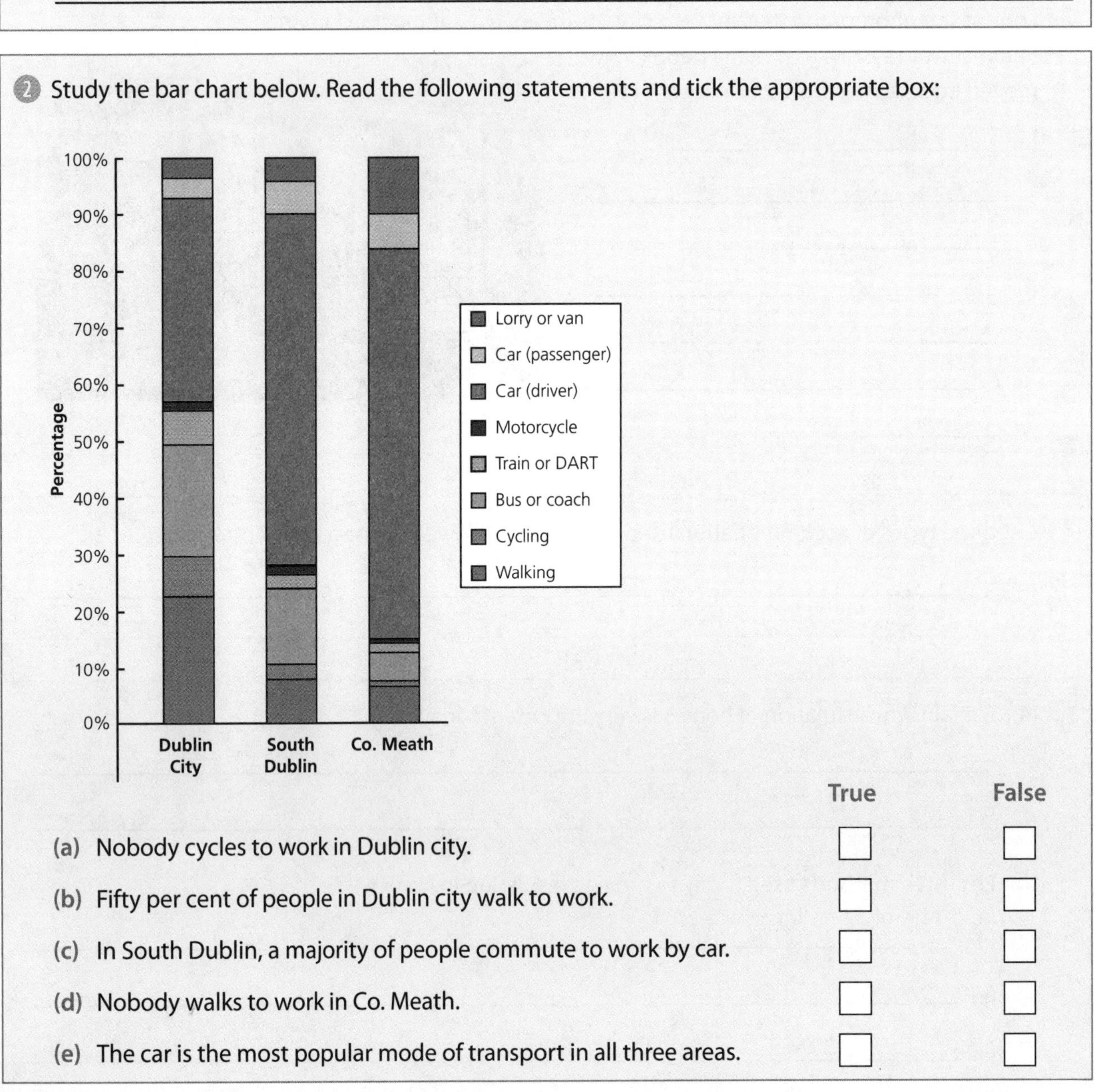

	True	False
(a) Nobody cycles to work in Dublin city.	☐	☐
(b) Fifty per cent of people in Dublin city walk to work.	☐	☐
(c) In South Dublin, a majority of people commute to work by car.	☐	☐
(d) Nobody walks to work in Co. Meath.	☐	☐
(e) The car is the most popular mode of transport in all three areas.	☐	☐

3 A journey to school survey

(a) Use a show of hands to find out the mode of transport used by pupils in your class to travel to school.

(b) Write in the numbers in the space provided below.

Mode of transport	
Car	
Rail/light rail	
Bus	
Bicycle	
Walking	

(c) Now draw bars on the chart below to show the results of your survey in the spaces provided.

Number of pupils

30

25

20

15

10

5

Car Rail/light rail Bus Bicycle Walking

10.6 Urban problems

1 The inner city refers to: (*Tick the correct box.*)

(a) An inland city in the centre of the country. ☐

(b) An old run-down area beside the CBD. ☐

(c) The centre of a satellite town. ☐

(d) The area of a city where people come to work every day. ☐

2 Fill the blank spaces with appropriate words in the following passage:

Several problems exist in the inner city. Some young ______________ find it ______________ to get work. Many young people leave __________ early and have no ______________ qualifications. They are less likely to be ____________________ literate. Therefore, jobs in the nearby ____________________ are beyond their ____________________.

As well as that, the inner cities offer little chance of work in manufacturing since industrial ________________ now tend to be _______________ on the city _______________ where sites are _______________.

Communities are under stress in the inner city because of crime. Much of the crime is ____________________. Inner cities have also seen _________________ disruption in recent times. This was because _________________ couples were given ____________________ in other parts of the city. These couples lost the ________________________ of their extended ________________________.

3 In the boxes provided, match each of the letters in column X with the number of its pair in column Y. One match has been made for you.

X		Y	
A	This part of the city is a zone of decline.	1	Leaving school early
B	This is a cause of inner-city crime.	2	The extended family
C	This limits young peoples' job opportunities in inner cities.	3	The drugs problem
D	This is an important social support for young parents.	4	The inner city

X	Y
A	☐
B	3
C	☐
D	☐

4 Which of the following describes urban sprawl? *(Tick the correct box.)*

(a) The development of urban transport routes. ☐

(b) Inner-city decline. ☐

(c) The spread of houses into the countryside. ☐

(d) The increase in the size of the CBD. ☐

5 Look at the cartoon below.

(a) Explain how urban sprawl disrupts the natural world.

____

____

(b) Suggest a suitable title for this cartoon.

____

10.7 Urban improvements

1 Study the sketch map of Dublin below, and write the appropriate name in the space provided.

(a) Dolphin's Barn
(b) Ballymun
(c) Tallaght
(d) Adamstown

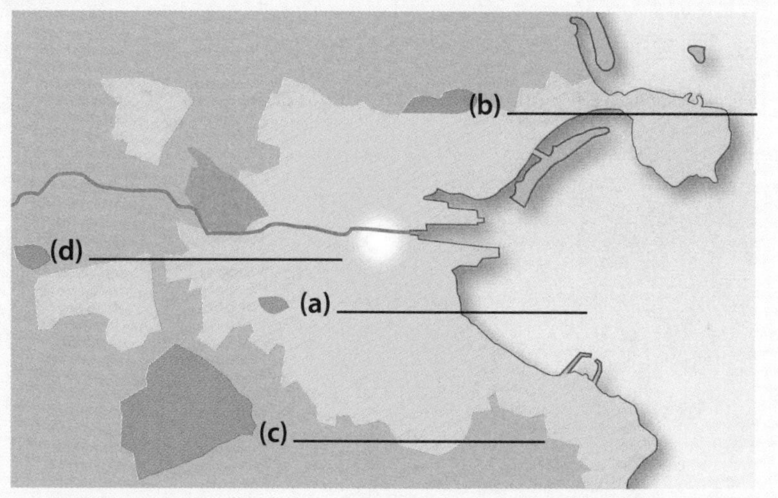

2 Explain the following terms.

- Urban renewal

___

___

___

- Urban redevelopment

___

___

___

3 (a) Name one example of urban renewal that you have studied.

___

(b) Explain two problems that existed in that community.

(i) ___

(ii) ___

(c) Explain two ways in which urban renewal is likely to improve the quality of life within the community.

(i) ___

___

(ii) ___

___

4 Circle the correct answer in each of the following statements:

(a) Tallaght has a *DART / Luas* terminal.

(b) Tallaght had *excellent services / poor services* from its beginnings.

(c) The Square in Tallaght is a *shopping centre / open park*.

5 Study the information on Adamstown below and answer the following questions.

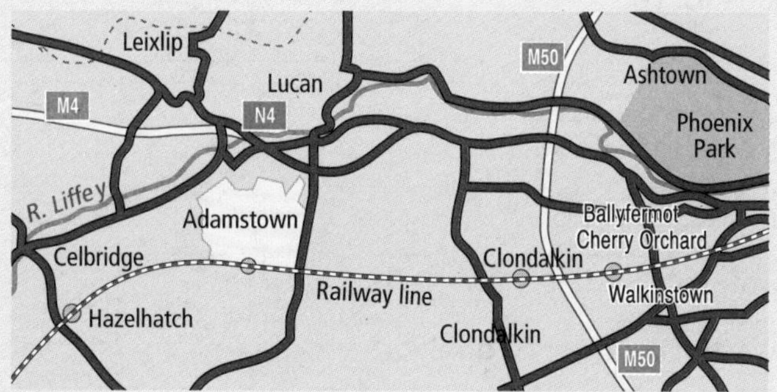

Adamstown is a new town 16 km west of Dublin city centre. Work began on the building of Adamstown in 2004.

Adamstown is located beside the Kildare-Heuston railway line. Heuston is on the Luas Red line where there are connections to Dublin's CBD.

Adamstown is a high-density development as most buildings have three floors. Residential density is a minimum of seventy-two houses per hectare. By mid-2008, 1,000 homes were occupied.

Unlike Tallaght in its early years, services were provided early. The train station, two QBCs, primary schools and crèche facilities were all in place by 2008. Local shopping centres were opened.

In 2008, planning permission was granted for Adamstown District Centre. This centre will include shops, offices, services, leisure facilities and 600 apartments. Up to 2,500 people will work there.

Thirty hectares have been set aside for leisure and sporting areas that include four parks.

(a) Where is Adamstown located? ______________________

(b) Describe the housing densities in Adamstown. ______________________

____

____

(c) Write down three services that were provided in Adamstown for the first residents.

(i) ______________________

(ii) ______________________

(iii) ______________________

10.8 Urbanisation in the developing world

1 Circle the correct answer in each of the following statements:

(a) In developing world cities, shantytowns are located in *city centres / city outskirts*.

(b) Shanty towns in Kolkata are called *favelas / bustees*.

(c) *All homes / some homes* in Kolkata have running water.

2 In the boxes provided, match each of the letters in column X with the number of its pair in column Y. One match has been made for you.

X		Y	
A	The name of a large green area in Kolkata.	1	Howrah
B	A wealthy suburb of Kolkata.	2	Cricket
C	A popular game in Kolkata.	3	The Maidan
D	This district is located west of the River Hooghly.	4	Salt Lake

X	Y
A	
B	4
C	
D	

3 Look at the sketch of a typical city in the developing world and answer the following questions.

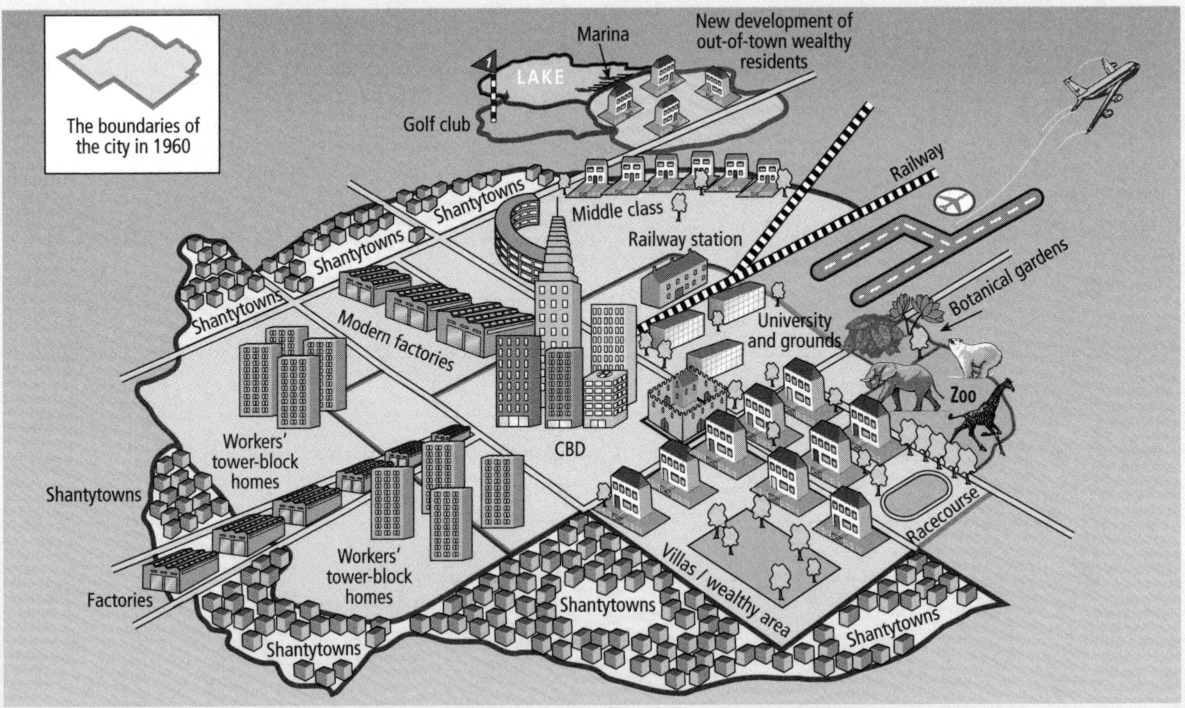

(a) Give one reason why shantytowns are located on the outskirts of the city.

___

(b) Why are workers' tower-block homes located near factories?

___

(c) Write down one way in which the picture highlights sharp social inequalities.

___

___

Revision crossword

Down

1 A lane reserved for buses and taxis
2 A very poor district on the edge of a city in a poor country
3 Dublin's first settlers
4 A famous manufacturing industry in Paris
7 A light rail system in Dublin
9 A suburb of Limerick with a large shopping centre
10 This is used to conserve heat in modern homes
12 The name of a large park in Kolkata
13 A coastal railway in Dublin
14 A major social problem in inner cities

Across

2 The uncontrolled spread of a city into the countryside
5 A means of discouraging illegal parking in towns and cities
6 A modern name for Calcutta
8 An airport beside Paris
11 A 21st century town west of Dublin city
13 A theme park near Paris
14 A supermarket chain found in Paris
15 A county council area in North Co. Dublin

Chapter 11

Primary Economic Activities

11.1 The Earth as a resource

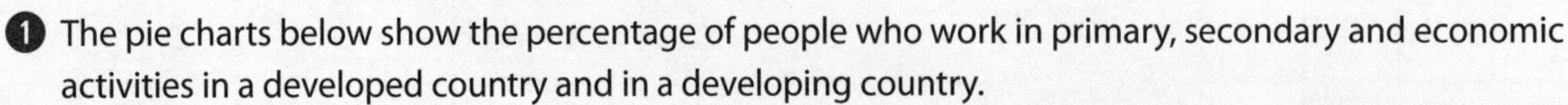

❶ The pie charts below show the percentage of people who work in primary, secondary and economic activities in a developed country and in a developing country.

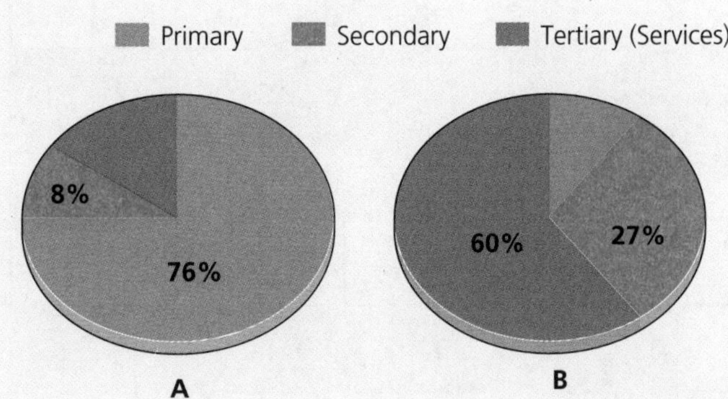

(a) Calculate the number of people who work in tertiary activities in country A.

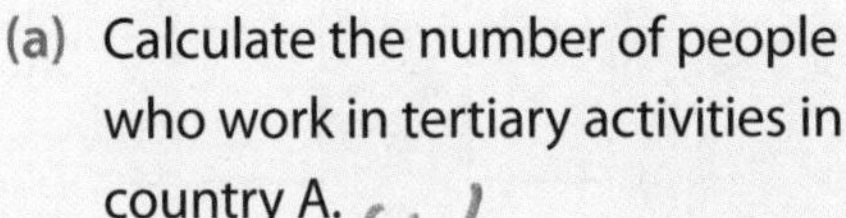

(b) Which pie chart represents a developed country?

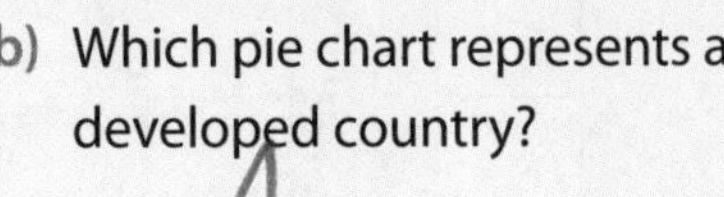

(c) Use the information in pie chart A to complete the bar chart below.

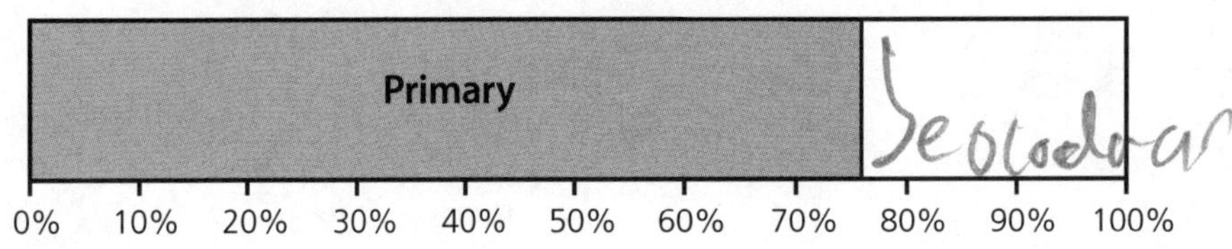

❷ Which of the following are all examples of people involved in primary activities?

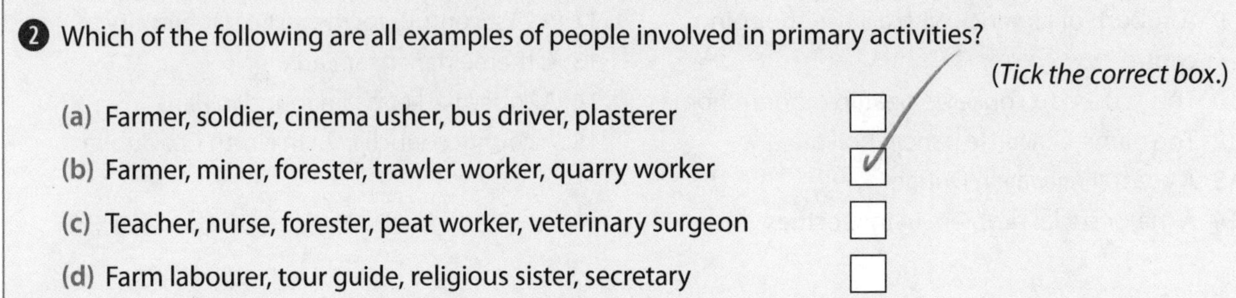

(Tick the correct box.)

(a) Farmer, soldier, cinema usher, bus driver, plasterer ☐

(b) Farmer, miner, forester, trawler worker, quarry worker ☐

(c) Teacher, nurse, forester, peat worker, veterinary surgeon ☐

(d) Farm labourer, tour guide, religious sister, secretary ☐

❸ Look at the list of resources in column 1. Write down in column 2 whether these resources are renewable or non-renewable.

	1	2
A	Water	Renewable
B	Timber	Renewable
C	Soil	R
D	Coal	N R
E	Gravel quarry	N N
F	Fish	R

11.2 Water as a resource

❶ Fill in the missing words in the following paragraph that describes the water cycle:

The heat of the sun evaporates seawater and turns it into a gas that is called water vapour. This gas rises and contend. When it cools, it ______ into ______ that make up clouds. As it cools further, it falls as rain. Water returns to the sea in river. This whole process is known as the water cycle.

❷ Look at the diagram below.

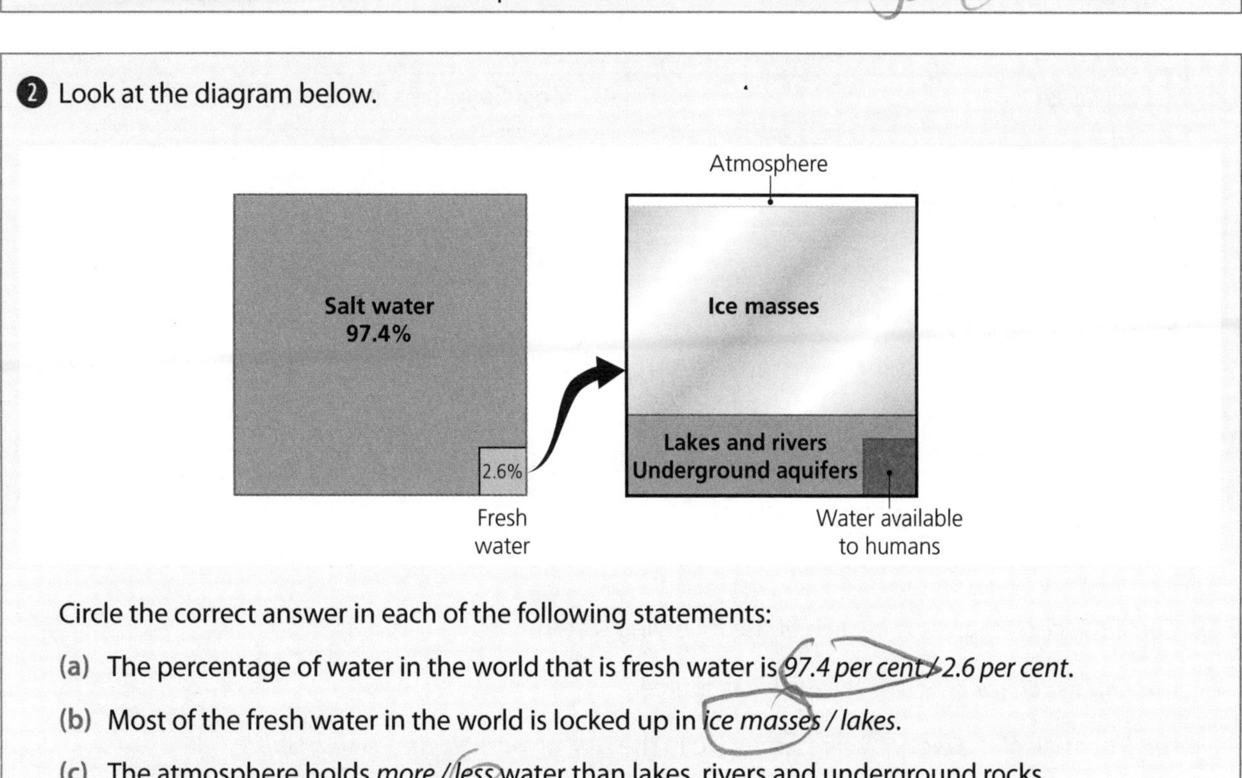

Circle the correct answer in each of the following statements:

(a) The percentage of water in the world that is fresh water is *97.4 per cent / 2.6 per cent*.

(b) Most of the fresh water in the world is locked up in *ice masses / lakes*.

(c) The atmosphere holds *more / less* water than lakes, rivers and underground rocks.

❸ Write down two ways through which people can conserve water.

(a) have less bottles

(b) called rain water

4 Look at the rainfall chart for Cairo and answer the following questions.

(a) Cairo receives no rainfall for how many months of the year?

____

(b) How many mms of rain falls on Cairo during the entire year?

____

Rainfall in mm

10

5

J F M A M J J A S O N D

Rainfall chart for Cairo

5 In the boxes provided, match each of the letters in column X with the number of its pair in column Y. One match has been made for you.

X		Y	
A	The floodplain of the Nile	1	77
B	The location of a dam	2	Aswan
C	Egypt's population in millions in 2005	3	Stores irrigation water
D	Lake Nasser	4	Most Egyptians live there

X	Y
A	
B	
C	1
D	

11.3 Oil: A finite resource

1 Circle the correct answer in each of the following statements:

(a) Oil is a *renewable / non-renewable* resource.

(b) The bulk of the world's oil reserves are in the *Gulf of Mexico / the Persian Gulf*.

(c) The Persian Gulf region is also known as the *Far East / Middle East*.

2 Look at the map of the Middle East and surrounding regions. Insert the following places on the map:

- Saudi Arabia
- Iraq
- Iran
- Kuwait
- The Red Sea
- Riyadh
- The Persian Gulf
- The Indian Ocean

3 Read the following passage and fill in the blanks with appropriate words:

The __________ industry has brought great changes to Saudi __________. Before the __________ of oil, the __________ of that country were mainly nomadic __________. Today, many people __________ in the oil industry and enjoy the benefits of an urban __________. The country has moved from poverty to __________ in a short __________. However, the culture of the country is very __________ to that of the culture of Europe and the __________. The religion of Saudi Arabia is __________.

4 **The search for oil in Irish waters**

In the boxes provided, match each of the letters in column X with the number of its pair in column Y. One match has been made for you.

X	Y
A This sea is rich in oil deposits.	1 The Porcupine Bank
B Gas is already coming ashore from this gas field.	2 Corrib Gas Field
C A gas find exists in this field off the coast of Mayo.	3 Kinsale Gas Field
D This sea area lies off the coast of Kerry.	4 The North Sea

X	Y
A	4
B	
C	
D	

11.4 The exploitation of Ireland's peatlands

1 Fill in the blank spaces in the sentence below:

Raised bogs are found mainly in the ____________ while blanket bogs are found in the ____________ of Ireland.

2 Why is it necessary to drain the bogs before they are exploited?

____

3 Why are the tyres that are used in bog machinery very wide?

____

4 Explain the function of each of the following machines that are used by Bord na Móna:

(a) A ditcher: ______________________________

(b) A grader: ______________________________

(c) A harrow: ______________________________

(d) A ridger: ______________________________

(e) A light railway: ______________________________

5 In the boxes provided, match each of the letters in column X with the number of its pair in column Y. One match has been made for you.

X	Y
A Traditional turf-cutting tool	1 Briquettes
B Domestic fuel	2 Bord na Móna
C Irish turf company	3 Compost
D Peat-based garden product	4 The sleán

X	Y
A	
B	
C	
D	3

11.5 Fishing

1 Explain the following terms:

- Overexploitation of fish

  Over fish

- Sustainable fishing

  fishing at a sustainable level

- Continental shelf

  area around island of fish plankton level

- Plankton

  small creatures fish eat

2 The bar chart shows landings of cod in Ireland in selected years. Study it and then circle the correct answers in each of the statements below.

(a) The figures show that catches of cod were *increasing / decreasing*.

(b) Fish stocks were declining due to *underfishing / overfishing*.

(b) The cod catch was *six times / four times* smaller in 2001 than in 1987.

Weight in thousands of tonnes

10

5

1987 1992 1996 2001

3 **(a)** Explain why in the past, fishermen in currachs were able to catch small amounts of fish only.

they had small nets

(b) List three items of modern technology that trawlers use to catch fish.

(i) sonar

(ii) Radar

(iii) Nets

4. Mark in and name the following fishing ports on the map of Ireland below: Howth, An Daingean (Dingle), Skerries, Killybegs, Castletownbere, Dunmore East. (You may need to use an atlas.)

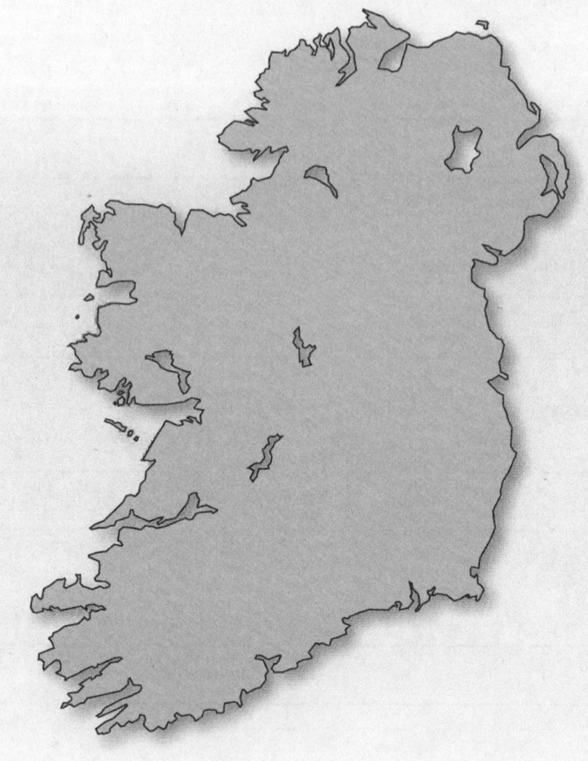

5. Match each of the letters in column X with the number of its pair in column Y. One match has been made for you.

X	Y
A This is a demersal species.	1 Sonar
B These are crustaceans.	2 Herring
C These are pelagic fish.	3 Cod
D This helps to detect fish shoals.	4 Lobster

X	Y
A	3
B	4
C	2
D	1

11.6 Farming

1 Place each of the items below into the correct column.

milking the cows, harvesting silage, veterinary services, milk, government grants, farmyard manure

Input	Process	Output
1 grants	1 milking cows	1 manure
2 veterary servises	2 harvesting silage	2 milk

2 Study the plan of a mixed farm shown below (not to scale) and answer the following questions.

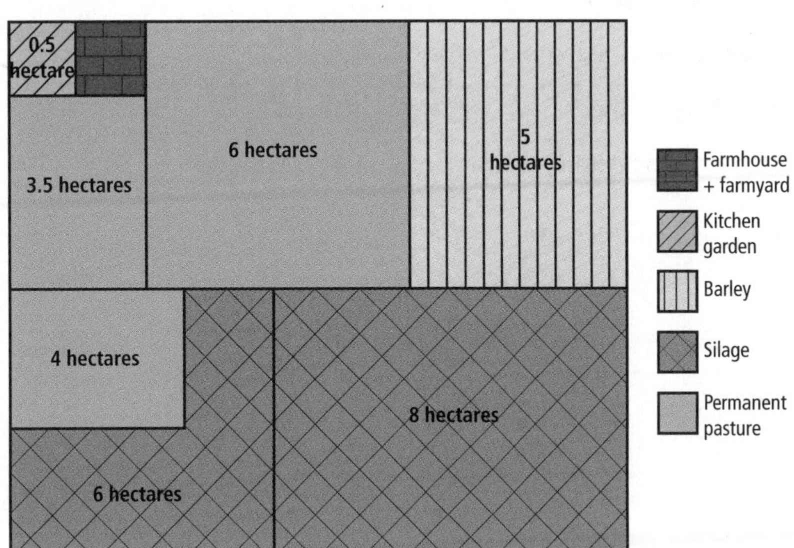

(a) How many hectares are used for silage and permanent pasture combined? 27.5 hectares

(b) Which takes up most land, barley or silage? Silage

(c) Why, do you think, is the kitchen garden close to the farmhouse?

so it okay to get to the house in case something going wrong.

CHAPTER 12

SECONDARY ECONOMIC ACTIVITIES

12.1 Building resources into products

1 Match each of the letters in column X with the number of its pair in column Y. One match has been made for you.

X	Y
A An input in a biscuit factory	1 Milk
B An output in a computer assembly factory	2 Flour
C An output in a timber joinery	3 PC
D An input in a dairy processing plant	4 Windows

X	Y
A	
B	
C	4
D	

2 The following is a list of **inputs** and **outputs** in a shoe factory. Write the words **input** or **output** as appropriate after each of the following items below.

Electricity:	______________	Sandals:	______________
Shoes:	______________	Waste leather:	______________
Labour:	______________	Shoeboxes:	______________
Leather:	______________	Canteen supplies:	______________
Glue:	______________	Boots:	______________

12.2 Factory location

❶ List the factors below that are important for the location of a factory. Two have been filled in for you.

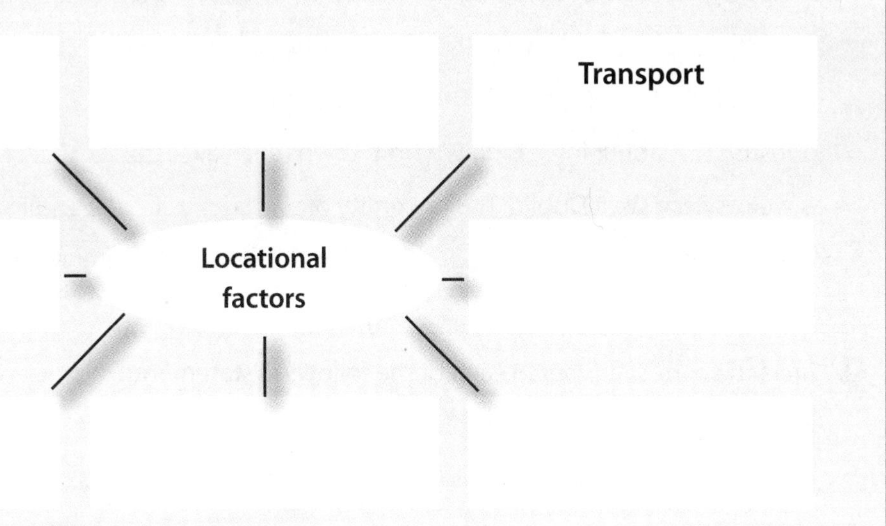

❷ Circle the correct answer in each of the following statements:

(a) When milk is processed into butter, it *gains / loses* volume.

(b) High-tech manufacturers regard the Irish workforce as *highly educated / poorly educated*.

(c) Baking causes inputs to *gain volume / lose volume* after processing.

❸ (a) What is an industrial estate?

____

____

____

(b) Explain one reason why many manufacturers choose to locate their plants in industrial estates.

____

____

____

(c) Explain one reason why light industries are located in industrial estates.

____

____

____

(d) Name one industrial estate in Ireland.

____

❹ Fill in the blank spaces with appropriate words:

Intel is located in a ________________ site in Leixlip, Co. ________________. The ________________ played a major role in encouraging the company to come to ____________________ through ____________________ and other tax incentives. More than ________________ of the workforce have third-level qualifications. The company manufactures ________________ for the computer industry. The labour force is drawn from towns such as ________________ and ____________________ as well as from West Dublin. The proximity of ____________________ airport is important for the company because ________________ are exported by air to markets in ____________________.

❺ Circle the correct answer in each of the following statements:

(a) RUSAL Alumina is an example of *light / heavy* industry.

(b) The resource material that is processed in the RUSAL plant is called *bauxite / alumina*.

(c) *Electricity / coal* is used to provide the energy for the plant.

❻ Fill in the blank spaces with appropriate words:

Rusal ________________ is located on the ________________ bank of the Shannon ______________ in Co. ______________. The plant is an alumina ______________. Bauxite, the resource ______________ is imported from West ____________________ .

The bauxite is transported to the plant in large ________________. The resource material is ________________ into a semi-________________ product called ________________. This product is exported to Scandinavia where it is ________________ into ________________.

12.3 Footloose industry

❶ Look at the photograph of the restored mill. Read the following statements and circle the correct answers.

(a) The mill was built in the *nineteenth century / twentieth century*.

(b) The source of power was *water / coal*.

(c) The mill manufactured *textiles / computers*.

❷ Match each of the letters in column X with the number of its pair in column Y. One match has been made for you.

X	Y
A Power source today.	1 Ring roads
B Power source in the nineteenth century.	2 Industrial estates
C Factories are located in these.	3 Coal
D Many factories and industrial estates are located beside these.	4 Electricity

X	Y
A	☐
B	☐
C	☐
D	1

❸ Fill in the blank spaces with appropriate words:

The Industrial Revolution began more than __________ years ago. Water power was quickly replaced by steam __________________. Since coal was used to create steam, factories became tied to ____________________. Therefore, manufacturing in the nineteenth century was not ___________________.

However, in the twentieth century electricity replaced ____________________ as the major power source. Workers became more _________________ as transport improved. Industrial ______________ were established beside towns and cities. Therefore, much modern _____________________ became ___________________.

❹ A modern factory is shown located on the edge of the city beside a motorway. Explain how each of the factors below is important to the location of that factory.

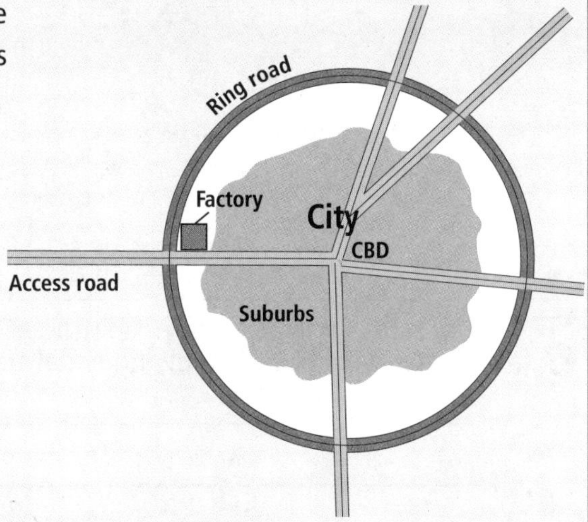

(a) Proximity to a labour force:

____

____

(b) Proximity to a ring road:

____

____

(c) A large site:

____

____

12.4 Industrial location: Change over time

❶ Fill in the blank spaces with appropriate words:

In the __________ century, iron works were small. They were located close to __________________ because charcoal from the forests was used to ________________ iron. Forests were quickly _______________________. A new energy source was needed. ___________________ became this new energy source. As ____________________ was very bulky, iron smelters moved from the edge of forests to the __________________. Iron smelters were ___________________ to coalfields for many generations. However, by the middle of the ____________________ century, iron and steel mills in Britain were in difficulty. This was due to the exhaustion of ________________________ and to _____________________ from _____________________ in countries such as __________________. In Britain, old inefficient steel mills on the coalfields were __________________ down. New mills were built on the ____________________. Sheffield is the only major inland steel _______________ today.

❷ On the map of Britain, insert and name the location of four present-day iron and steel mills.

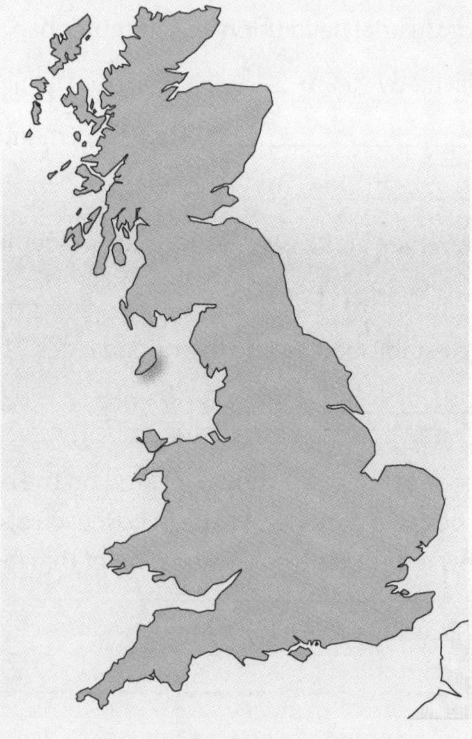

❸ (a) What is meant by the term industrial inertia?

____

____

(b) Name one location in Britain where industrial inertia in the steel industry exists.

____

4 Link each term in column X with its matching pair in column Y. One has been done for you.

X		Y	
A	This city is still a steel producer.	1	After 1960
B	In the eighteenth century, this was the energy source for ironworks.	2	Industrial inertia
C	Inland steelworks in Britain began to lose money at this time.	3	Charcoal
D	Industry might not relocate even though it would be economically sound to do so.	4	Japan
E	This country produced cheaper steel than Britain.	5	Sheffield

X	Y
A	
B	
C	1
D	
E	

12.5 The role of women in industry

1 Study the the pie chart below and transfer the information in the pie chart to the diagram.

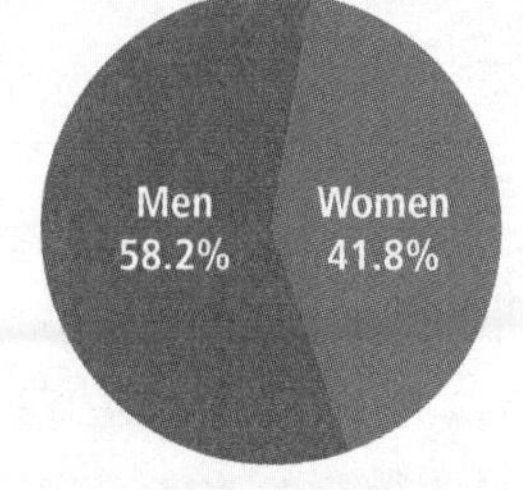

Ireland's workforce in 2005: male / female

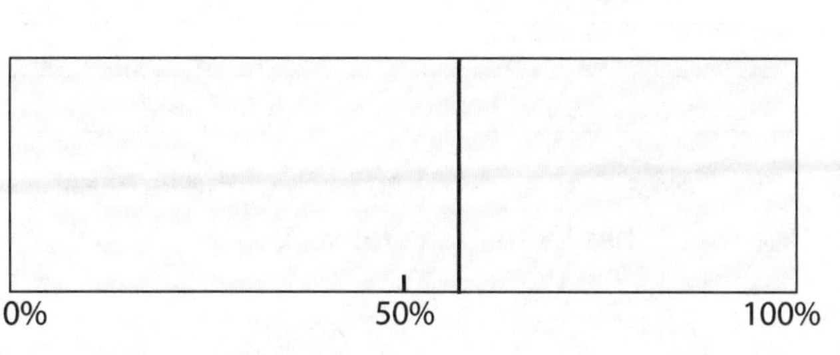

2 Study the information shown in the bar chart and circle the correct answers in the following sentences.

(a) The number of women at work in 1971 was *more than / less than* a quarter of a million.

(b) The number of women at work in 2006 was *more than / less than* one million.

(c) The number of women at work in 2006 was more than *three times / four times* greater than in 1971.

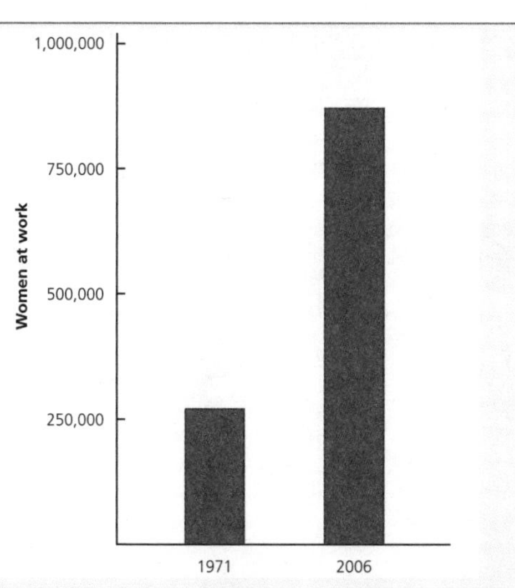

3 Study the information below and answer the following questions.

(a) What is meant by family-friendly policies?

____

____

____

____

(b) Write down three family-friendly options that are available for workers today.

(i) ______________________

(ii) ______________________

(iii) ______________________

(c) How can family-friendly policies benefit both employers and employees?

Benefits for employees:

____

____

Benefits for employers:

____

____

4 In the boxes provided, match each of the letters in column X with the number of its pair in column Y. One match has been made for you.

	X		Y
A	Millions of Chinese women work in these.	1	Repetitive tasks
B	Women's life expectancy in China has now reached this figure.	2	Large apartment blocks
C	Chinese workers live in these.	3	75 years
D	Chinese women perform these tasks in factories.	4	Export processing zones

X	Y
A	4
B	
C	
D	

5 Circle the correct answer in each of the following statements:

(a) Chinese workers earn *more than / less than* Irish workers.

(b) Millions of Chinese workers have moved *to the coast of China / to the interior of China* in search of work.

(c) Mothers in China today have *several children / one child* each.

12.6 Manufacturing on a world scale

1 Look at the map below and answer the following questions:

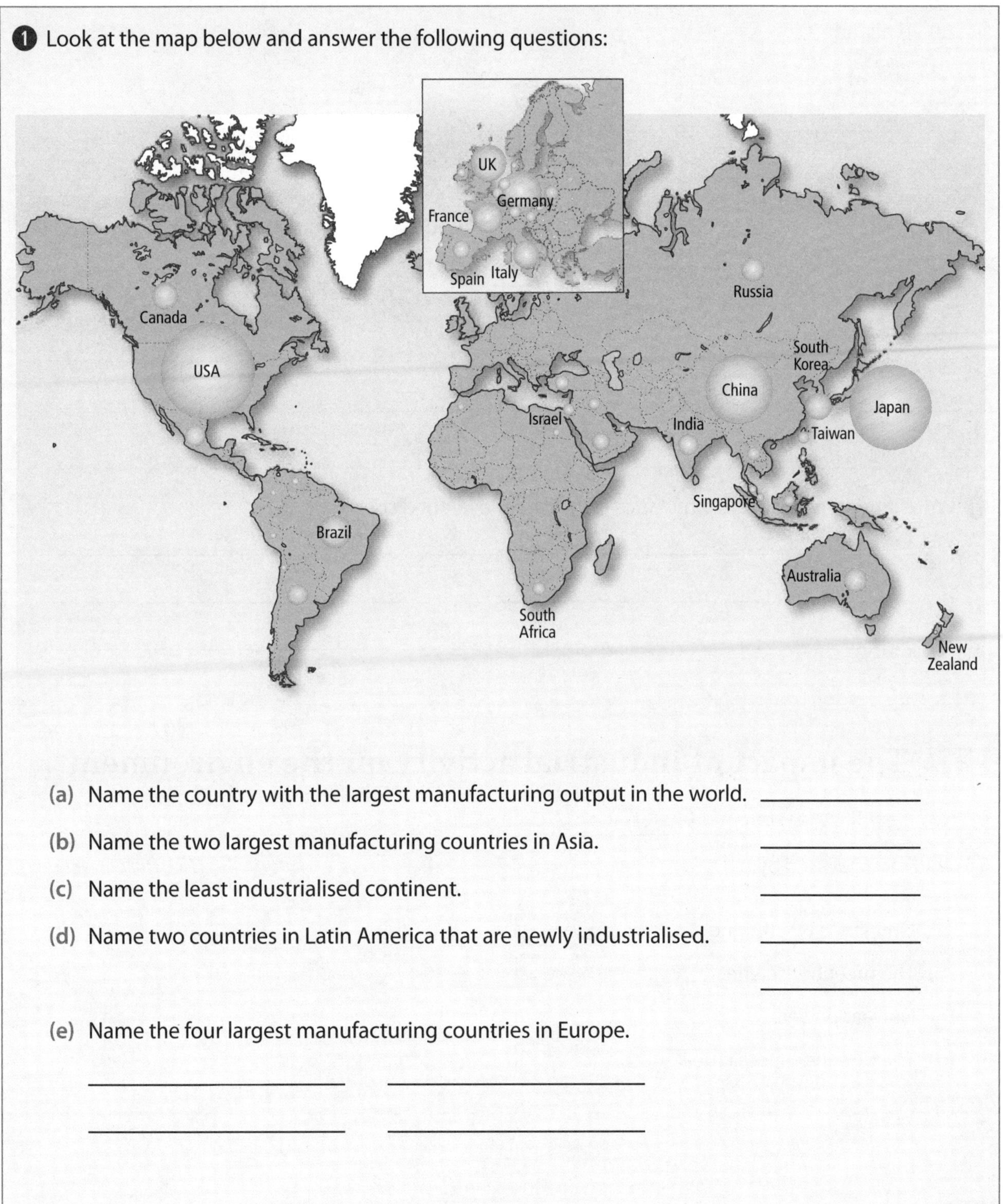

(a) Name the country with the largest manufacturing output in the world. ____________

(b) Name the two largest manufacturing countries in Asia. ____________

(c) Name the least industrialised continent. ____________

(d) Name two countries in Latin America that are newly industrialised. ____________

____

(e) Name the four largest manufacturing countries in Europe.

____________ ____________

____________ ____________

❷ Look at the map and write in the names of the following countries that have become industrialised in recent decades.

(a) South Korea
(b) Taiwan
(c) China
(d) Vietnam
(e) Thailand

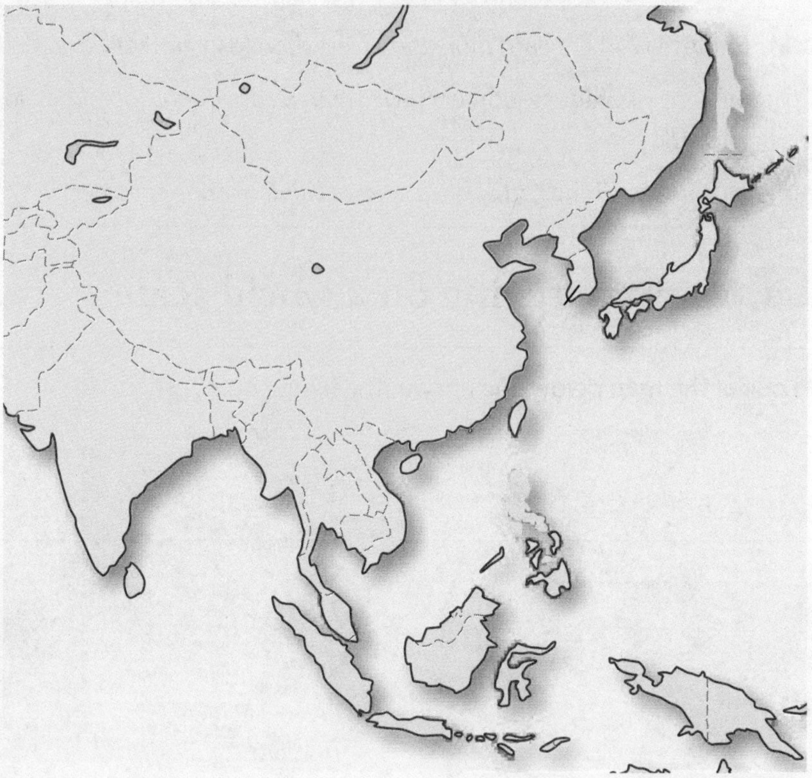

❸ Write down three reasons why Africa is the least-developed continent.

(a) ______________________________

(b) ______________________________

(c) ______________________________

12.7 The impact of industrial activity on the environment

❶ Acid rain is caused by: (*Tick the correct box*).

(a) Limestone weathering ☐
(b) The greenhouse effect ☐
(c) Nuclear power ☐
(d) The burning of fossil fuels ☐

❷ Study the map of Europe and answer the following questions:

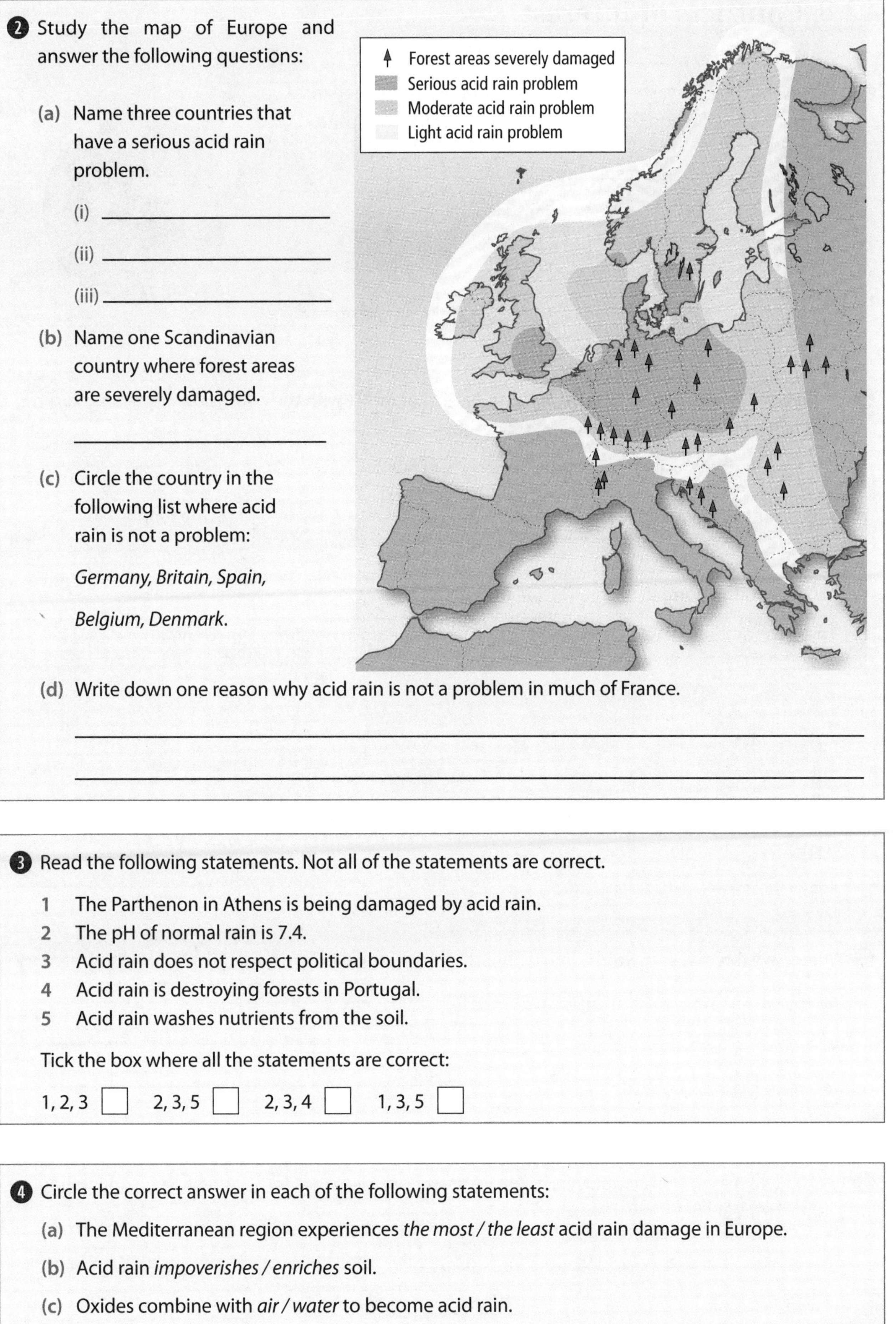

(a) Name three countries that have a serious acid rain problem.

(i) ____________________

(ii) ____________________

(iii) ____________________

(b) Name one Scandinavian country where forest areas are severely damaged.

____

(c) Circle the country in the following list where acid rain is not a problem:

Germany, Britain, Spain,

Belgium, Denmark.

(d) Write down one reason why acid rain is not a problem in much of France.

____

____

❸ Read the following statements. Not all of the statements are correct.

1 The Parthenon in Athens is being damaged by acid rain.
2 The pH of normal rain is 7.4.
3 Acid rain does not respect political boundaries.
4 Acid rain is destroying forests in Portugal.
5 Acid rain washes nutrients from the soil.

Tick the box where all the statements are correct:

1, 2, 3 ☐ 2, 3, 5 ☐ 2, 3, 4 ☐ 1, 3, 5 ☐

❹ Circle the correct answer in each of the following statements:

(a) The Mediterranean region experiences *the most / the least* acid rain damage in Europe.

(b) Acid rain *impoverishes / enriches* soil.

(c) Oxides combine with *air / water* to become acid rain.

12.8 Conflicts of interest

❶ Look at the table of waste management below for the Netherlands.
Include the information from the table in the pie chart opposite.

Waste management	
Landfill	4%
Recycling	64%
Incineration	32%

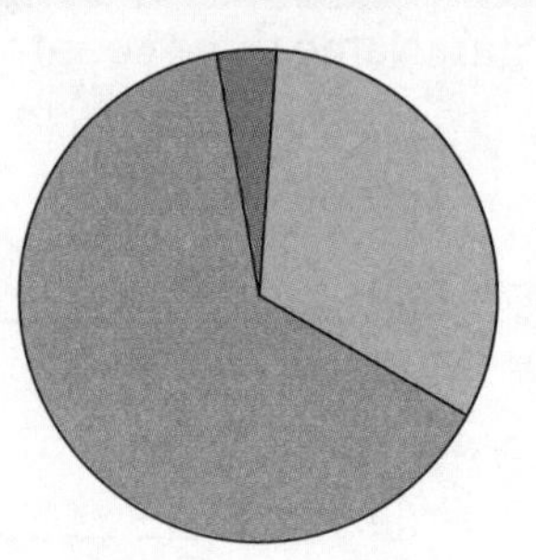

❷ In the boxes provided, match each of the letters in column X with the number of its pair in column Y.
One match has been made for you.

X		Y	
A	This country incinerates 55% of its waste.	1	One tonne
B	Ireland is running out of these.	2	Eleven
C	Ireland had this number of small incinerators in 2007.	3	Landfill sites
D	This is the amount of waste per person per year produced in Ireland.	4	Denmark

X	Y
A	☐
B	☐
C	2
D	☐

❸ Write down three ways in which working hours for workers were shortened over the twentieth century.

(a) ______________________

(b) ______________________

(c) ______________________

❹ Explain two reasons why employers might resist workers' demands for shortening of working hours.

(a) ______________________

(b) ______________________

Revision crossword

Down

1 Manufacturing plants that are not tied to a particular location
2 A bulky resource material in dairy processing
3 A major city in China
5 Regions to which many iron mills were tied in the past
6 A steel mill in South Wales that closed in 2001
7 A power station in the Shannon Estuary
9 A country in South-east Asia with low labour costs
12 An agency that encourages companies to locate in Ireland

Across

2 An output in the Intel plant
4 An input provided by workers
5 A fuel, derived from wood, which was used to smelt iron
8 An input in a factory
10 A community to which the Republic of Ireland belongs
11 The location of the Intel plant in Ireland
13 A continent with very little manufacturing
14 A new town in the West of Ireland with a large industrial estate
15 Output from a dairy factory

Chapter 13

Tertiary Economic Activities

13.1 Services

❶ Match each of the letters in column X with the number of its pair in column Y. One match has been made for you.

X		Y	
A	Administrative services	1	Mechanics
B	Repair services	2	Bank officials
C	Retail services	3	Civil servants
D	Financial services	4	Supermarket employees

X	Y
A	
B	
C	4
D	

13.2 Tourism

❶ On the lines numbered (i), (ii), (iv), label the divided rectangle below using the information shown in the table. Two labels have been added for you.

Visitors to Ireland, 2006	
Mainland Britain	48%
Rest of Europe	26%
North America	13%
Northern Ireland	8.6%
Other	4.4%

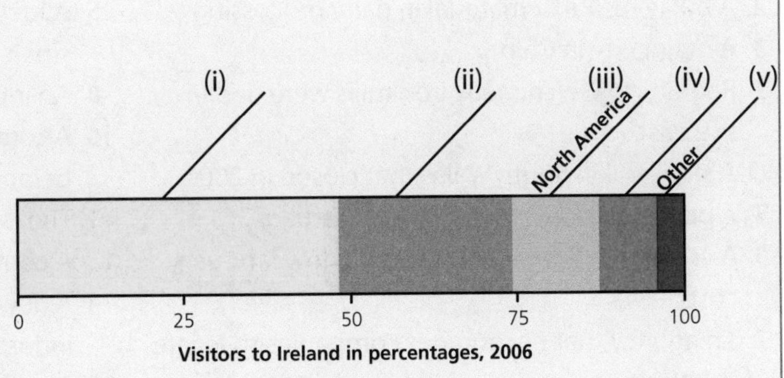

❷ Identify the county of each of the following locations in Ireland.

Scenic area	County
Gougánbarra	
Glendalough	
The Glen of Aherlow	
The Cliffs of Moher	

❸ Draw a map of your county in your copybook.

(a) Include and name the main urban areas.

(b) Write in the names of two areas in your county that are tourist attractions.

(c) In the case of each of the two tourist attractions that you have named, explain why tourists visit them.

❹ Suppose that you are in charge of a TV advertising campaign designed to encourage American tourists to come to Ireland. Compose a fifty-word voice-over for that advertisement.

____

____

____

____

❺ (a) Explain the term 'niche tourism'.

____

(b) Give one example of niche tourism that visitors enjoy in Ireland.

____

13.3 Tourism in Europe

❶ Look at the table showing the number of days when rain falls in the Costa del Sol in Southern Spain for the twelve months of the year. Complete the chart below with the appropriate number of wet days. (Two months have been done for you.)

Jan	Feb	Mar	Apr	May	Jun	Jul	Aug	Sep	Oct	Nov	Dec
7	6	5	5	3	1	0	0	2	4	6	6

Days of measurable rain in the Costa del Sol (0.2 mm or more)

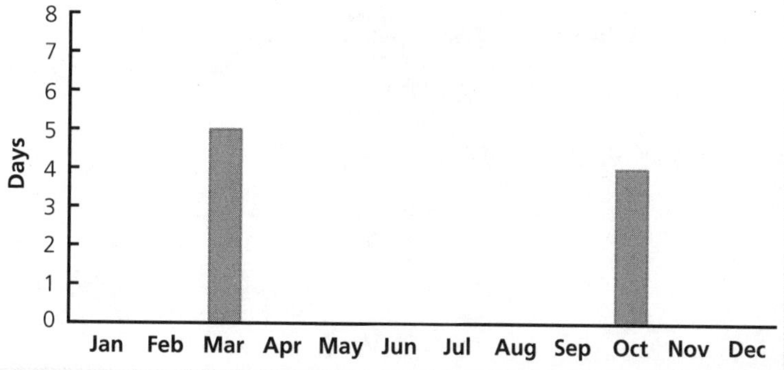

2 Fill in the blank spaces with appropriate words:

Mass tourism developed in Spain after the year __________. Tourists come to Spain from Northern ________________ because of high summer ____________________ and ______________.

Favourite holiday coasts include the ____. Millions of tourists also holiday on Spanish islands in the Mediterranean that include ______________ and ____________________. Tourism now accounts for one in __________ jobs in the Spanish economy.

3 How do the following groups benefit from tourism in Spain?

(a) Farmers

____

(b) Construction workers

____

(c) Local landowners

____

13.4 Tourism and transport links

1 (a) On the map of Spain below, mark in the following east-coast tourist centres: Barcelona, Valencia, Alicante, Malaga.

(b) On the map of Spain draw and name the E15 motorway along the Mediterranean coast of Spain.

(c) On the map below write the words 'Costa del Sol', where that stretch of coast is located.

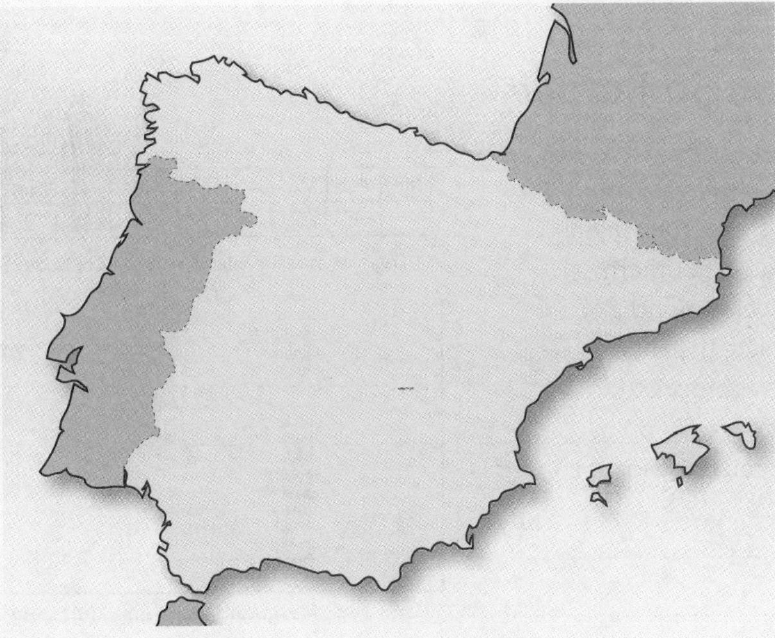

2 Look at the map of Spain and its island resorts below.

(a) Write down the collective name for the Spanish islands in the Mediterranean.

___

(b) Write down the collective name for the Spanish islands that are west of the coast of Africa.

___

(c) Explain why air transport is vital to the tourist industry in those groups of islands.

___

___

___

___

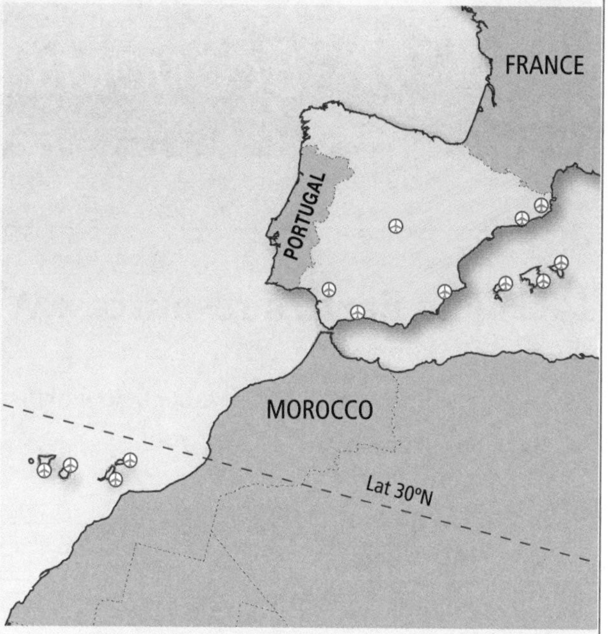

FRANCE

PORTUGAL

MOROCCO

Lat 30°N

13.5 The impact of tourism

1 Examine the photograph of Benidorm below and answer the following questions.

(a) Why do tourists visit this resort?

___

___

___

(b) How has the coastal landscape been changed by tourism?

___

___

___

(c) Explain two advantages and two disadvantages of tourism for local residents in resorts such as this.

Advantages

(i) ___

(ii) ___

Disadvantages

(i) ___

(ii) ___

Chapter 14

Economic Inequality

14.1 The Earth's resources: Who benefits?

❶ Using the information in the table below of Incomes for various countries, complete the following bar chart. One bar is drawn for you.

Income for various countries	
Country	**GDP per person in US$**
Denmark	51,074
USA	43,562
Brazil	5,640
Bulgaria	3,956
Bangladesh	437
Uganda	346

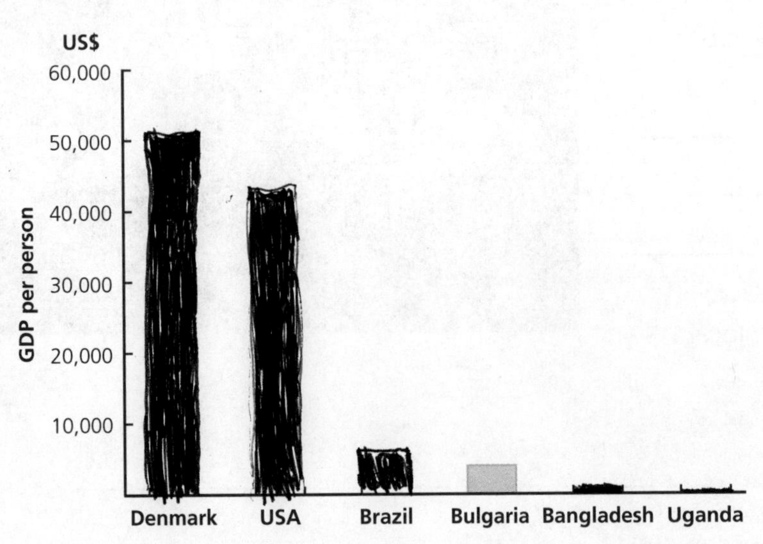

2 Study the map of the developed and developing world and answer the following questions:

M
C
B

The developed world
The quickly developing world
The slowly developing world
Border between North and South

(a) Write the names of the three countries in Latin America that are marked M, B, C.

M Mangua ____________________

B Brazil ____________________

C Colombia ____________________

(b) Name the sea that divides Southern Europe from Africa. ____________________

(c) Name three countries in South Asia that are slowly developing.

(i) ____________________

(ii) ____________________

(iii) ____________________

(d) Name two countries in East Asia that are in the developed world.

(i) ____________________

(ii) ____________________

(e) Name three countries in North Africa that are in the quickly developing world.

(i) ____________________

(ii) ____________________

(iii) ____________________

3 Study the chart comparing the Republic of Ireland with South Africa.

	Republic of Ireland	South Africa
Area	70,273 km²	1,221,037 km²
Population	4.3 million	48.5 million
GDP per capita US$	51,665 (2006)	5,133 (2006)
Life expectancy	78.5 years	50 years
Infant mortality rate	4.9 per 1,000	44.8 per 1,000
Maternal mortality per 100,000 pregnancies	2	150
Percentage population under 15	20%	32.6%
Internet users per 100 inhabitants	34.1 (2006)	10.8 (2006)

(a) Select from the table three statistics that show that South Africa is less developed than the Republic of Ireland.

(i) GDP per Capita

(ii) Life expectanse

(iii) Internet users.

(b) Use the bar chart to illustrate life expectancy in the Republic of Ireland and South Africa.

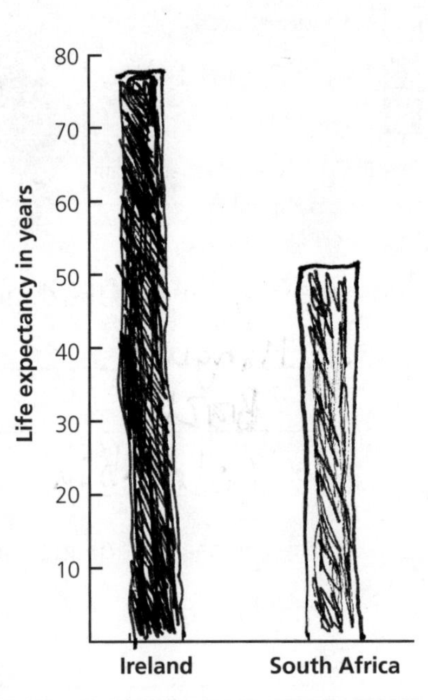

(c) Why is maternal mortality so high in South Africa?

____

____

____

____

____

4 Fill the spaces below with appropriate words.

In slowly developing countries, most people are working in the primary sector as _______________, fishermen and ____________________.

In quickly developing countries, the ____________________ sector declines in importance as more people work in the ____________________ and ____________________ sectors of the economy.

In developed countries, more than 50 per cent of the population is working in the ____________________ sector.

5 (a) Name the world's poorest region. ____________________

(b) Name three slowly developing countries in Africa that are landlocked.

(i) ____________________ (ii) ____________________ (iii) ____________________

(c) Suggest one way that being landlocked in Africa may hinder a country's development.

____

(d) Write down three other characteristics of the world's poorest countries

(i) ____________________

(ii) ____________________

(iii) ____________________

14.2 Exploitation of poor countries by wealthy countries

1 (a) Name two European countries that established colonies in Latin America in earlier centuries.

(i) ____________________ (ii) ____________________

(b) Name two European countries that established colonies in Africa in the nineteenth century.

(i) ____________________ (ii) ____________________

(c) Explain one reason why Africa was colonised by European countries in the past.

____

____

2 Match each of the letters in column X with the number of its pair in column Y. One match has been made for you.

X	Y
A Ireland exported these to Britain.	1 Kerrygold
B These were cut for charcoal.	2 800,000
C The number who died in the Great Famine.	3 Munster forests
D An Irish butter brand today.	4 Live cattle

X	Y
A	4
B	3
C	2
D	1

3 Study the map below and answer the following questions:

MAURITANIA
iron ore
LIBYA
crude oil
EGYPT
crude oil
ETHIOPIA
cocoa / coffee
NIGER
uranium
CHAD
cotton
GUINEA
bauxite
NIGERIA
crude oil
COTE D'IVOIRE
coffee
GHANA
cocoa
KENYA
coffee
EQUATORIAL GUINEA
cocoa
ZAMBIA
copper
ANGOLA
crude oil
BOTSWANA
diamonds
MALAWI
tobacco

(a) Name three agricultural raw materials that are exported from Africa.

(i) Coffee

(ii) tabalco

(iii) __________

(b) Name three minerals that Africa produces.

(i) iron ore

(ii) diamonds

(iii) bauxtbe

4 Name a country that produces coffee in each of the regions below:

(a) A Latin American country: __________

(b) An African country: __________

(c) An Asian country: __________

5 Explain two reasons why coffee-producing countries make very little money from the coffee business.

(a) __________

(b) __________

14.3 Aid to the South

❶ In the boxes provided, match each of the letters in column X with the number of its pair in column Y. One match has been made for you.

X		Y	
A	Bottled water, medicines, food.	1	Bilateral aid
B	Many countries give aid to a central agency.	2	NGOs
C	Bóthar, Concern, Trócaire.	3	Multilateral aid
D	Aid given by one country to another.	4	Emergency aid

X	Y
A	4
B	3
C	2
D	1

❷ Circle the correct answer in each of the following statements:

(a) A country that provides aid is known as a *donor / recipient* country.

(b) Aid that is given in response to a natural disaster is known as *tied aid / emergency aid.*

(c) Aid that helps people to help themselves gives these people *a dependent mentality / self-reliance.*

❸ Fill in the blank spaces with appropriate words:

Ethiopia is an example of a country that ____________________ from Ireland's ________________ aid programme.

Irish aid in Ethiopia has been invested in boring ____________________ for rural ____________.
As a result, the villagers now have water to ____________________ their fields. Farmers can grow ____________________ crops of food a year. They can sell their surplus ____________________ in nearby ____________________. Farmers are now in a position to ____________________ their children. This gives their children choices that their ____________________ never had. It helps young people to break out of ____________________.

14.4 Factors that hinder economic development

1 On the map of Sudan and surrounding countries, mark in and name the following:

- The name of two neighbouring countries
- The Red Sea
- The capital city of Sudan
- The province of Darfur

R. Nile

2 Circle the correct answer in each of the following statements:

(a) Sudan has *high / low* population growth.

(b) Sudan has *one racial group / two racial groups of people*.

(c) The Sudanese government spends *more / less* on arms than it does on education.

3 (a) Explain one way in which rapid population growth contributes to desertification in Sudan.

____

____

____

(b) Explain one way in which spending on weapons hinders development in Sudan.

____

____

____

(c) How has civil war caused Sudan's national debt to increase?

____

____

____

14.5 Economic inequalities within the EU

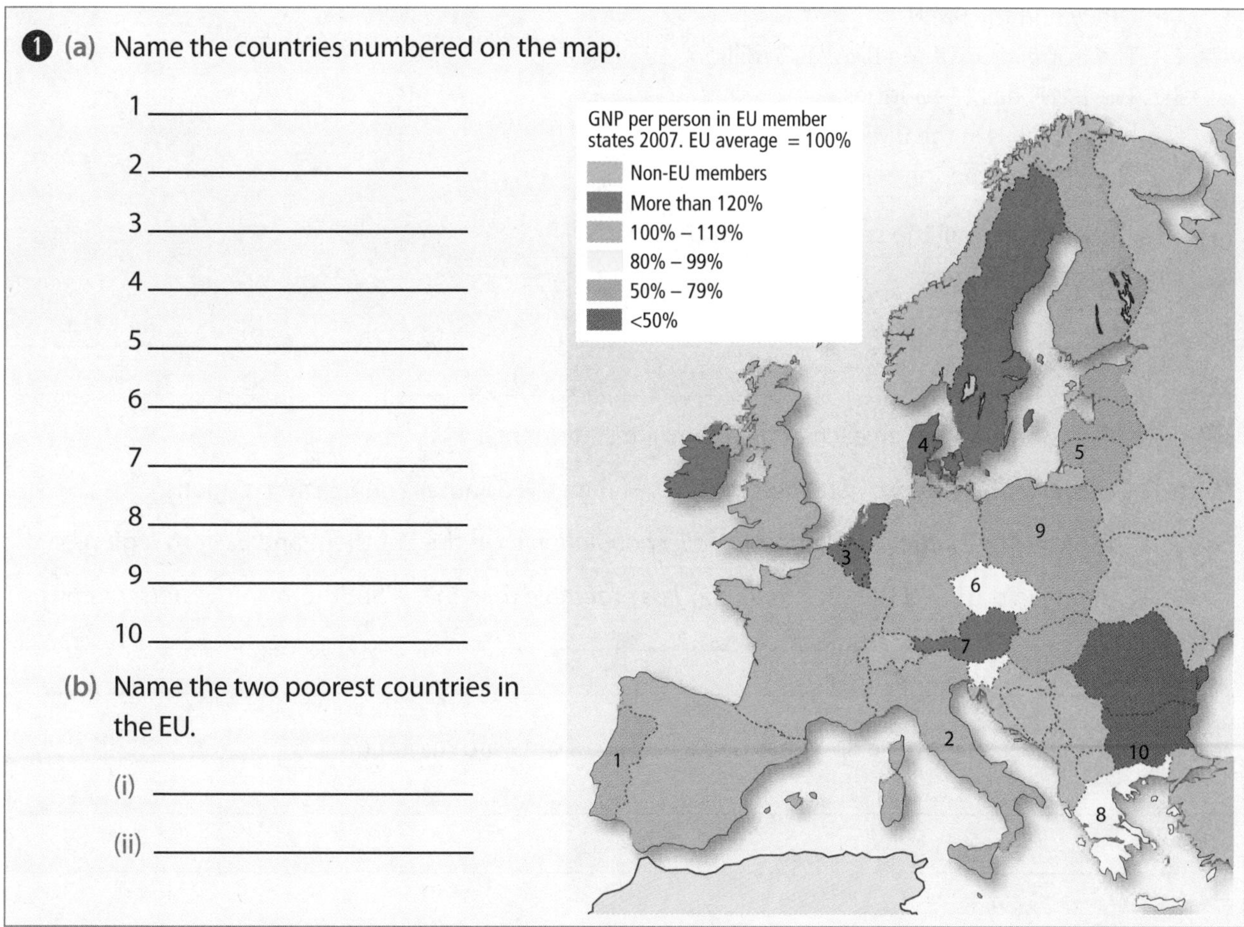

1 (a) Name the countries numbered on the map.

1 ______________________

2 ______________________

3 ______________________

4 ______________________

5 ______________________

6 ______________________

7 ______________________

8 ______________________

9 ______________________

10 ______________________

(b) Name the two poorest countries in the EU.

(i) ______________________

(ii) ______________________

2 The Border, Midlands and Western Regions

Look at the map of Ireland and complete the following questions. (You may need to consult a map of Ireland.)

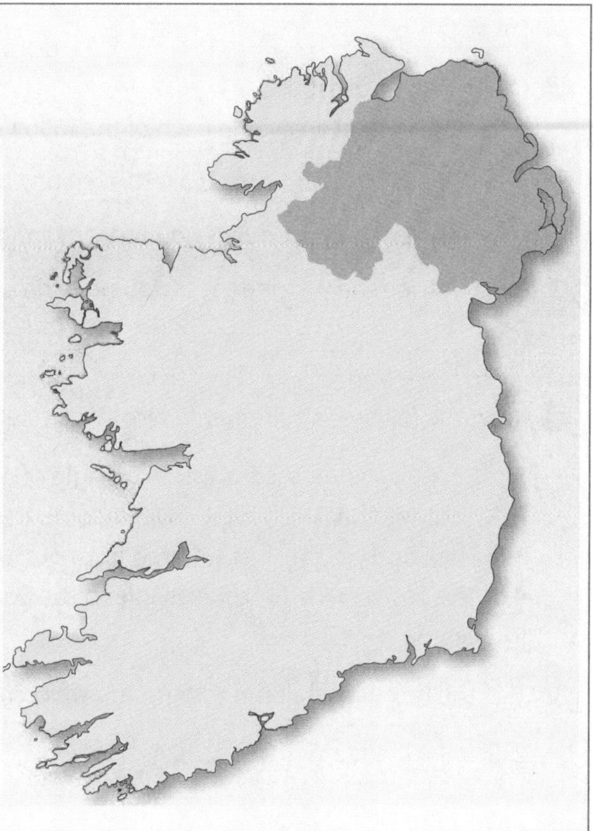

(a) Draw the boundary between the BMW and the Southern and Eastern Regions.

(b) Shade in the BMW and name it.

(c) How many counties are in the BMW?

____

(d) How many Leinster counties are in the BMW?

____

(e) Name the five border counties of the BMW.

____

____

____

3 Read the following statements. Not all the statements are correct.

1 Offaly is in the BMW.
2 The population of the BMW is 3 million.
3 The BMW has 14 counties.
4 Monaghan is in the BMW.
5 The BMW is a peripheral region.

Tick the box where all the statements are correct:

2, 3, 5 ☐ 1, 3, 5 ☐ 2, 3, 4 ☐ 1, 4, 5 ☐

4 Circle the correct answer in each of the following statements:

(a) The BMW is *more prosperous / less prosperous* than the Southern and Eastern regions.

(b) The BMW has a *larger population / smaller population* than the Southern and Eastern regions.

(c) Farming in the BMW is *more profitable / less profitable* than in the Southern and Eastern regions.

5 Explain one reason why the BMW has had a history of outward migration.

____

____

____

6 North and South Italy

Circle the correct answer in each of the following statements:

(a) The plain of Lombardy is a *fertile region / infertile region*.

(b) Northern Italy produces *abundant hydroelectricity / no hydroelectricity*.

(c) Southern Italy experiences a *summer drought / summer rainfall*.

7 Read the following statements. Not all the statements are correct.

1 Rome is part of the industrial triangle of northern Italy.
2 Southern Italians have a lower income than people in the North of Italy.
3 The South of Italy has suffered from outward migration.
4 The *Cassa* made funds available to the South of Italy.
5 Genoa is in Sicily.

Tick the box where all the statements are correct:

2, 3, 5 ☐ 1, 2, 5 ☐ 2, 3, 4 ☐ 1, 4, 5 ☐

8 (a) Look at the following list of manufacturing companies. Circle the two that are **not** Italian.
- Audi
- Gucci
- FIAT
- Zanussi
- Benetton
- Renault

(b) Look at the Italian cities listed below. Circle the one city that is **not** in northern Italy.
- Venice
- Milan
- Genoa
- Naples
- Turin

9 Fill the spaces below with appropriate words.

Agricultural output is ____________________ in the Po valley of northern Italy.

Southern Italy has suffered from ____________________ migration. Southern Italy is also known as the ____________________.

The islands of ____________________ and ____________________ are part of Italy.

Incomes in ____________________ Italy are lower than in ____________________ Italy.

The great motorway to the South of Italy is known as the ____________________.

14.6 Ending economic inequality

1 (a) Explain the term 'kleptocrats'.

____

(b) Give one example of appropriate aid to the South.

____

2 Explain the aim of the Fairtrade Movement.

____

____

3 Explain one reason why many developing world countries are in debt.

____

____

4 Explain one way in which high foreign debt affects the lives of children in poor countries.

____

____

5 Write down two sentences about the Make Poverty History Campaign.

____

____

Revision crossword

Down

1 An Irish butter brand
2 Barriers to trade
3 A burden that cripples many poor countries
6 A tourist attraction near Mount Vesuvius in southern Italy
7 An African country that exports bauxite
8 Zambia's most important export
9 One of Ireland's partner countries in Africa
11 An island that is part of Italy
13 A major coffee producer in South America
14 An Irish popstar who is helping to reduce poor countries' debts
15 A poor country in South-east Asia

Across

3 A war-torn province in Sudan
4 The poorest continent
5 A country's gross national product
7 An Italian manufacturer of leather goods
10 A city in the South of Italy
12 A river that flows through Sudan
14 Official aid from one country to another
16 A river in northern Italy
17 A major health problem, especially in Africa